"After reading Dr. Gould's earlier book, *Being Christian in the Twenty-First Century*, I was pleased to review this newest book and highly encourage my church clergy and other leaders to read it. Sam's writing is an accessible, concise systematic Christian ecclesiology that lends itself, with chapter-ending questions for reflection, to small group study."

—Steve Burnett, Retired District Superintendent, United Methodist Church, Colorado Springs

"Sam Gould's theological memoir, *An Open Christianity*, distills a lifetime of scholarly study, thoughtful reflection, ethical practice, and the creative weaving of complex biblical and theological ideas. He recounts his journey toward becoming an 'open Christian,' embracing the image of a loving Jesus and a faith unbound by rigid creeds or institutional constraints. With clarity and precision, Gould challenges exaggerated claims and problematic dogmas, advocating for a transformative reformation. Drawing on the finest scholarship, he speaks as a lay theologian with a personal credo that urges readers to reconsider our shifting culture, the decline in church commitment, and the dangerous mythology of Christian nationalism. This is a volume that will endure, rewarding those who seriously engage with it, by enriching their minds, uplifting their spirits, and calling them to new adventures in faith and life."

—Donald E. Messer, President Emeritus, Iliff School of Theology, Denver

"Sam Gould has combined decades of study, small group facilitation, and church leadership to provide a thoughtful expression of today's problems facing Christianity. *An Open Christianity* is well suited for small group study, providing a compelling and fresh perspective on faith that avoids the stumbling blocks of supernaturalism and outmoded beliefs that have turned many away from Christianity in recent years."

—Donald Lamm, MD, Research Professor, College of Medicine, University of Arizona

"Gould has beautifully and thoughtfully integrated his many years of reading and personal study into a very timely and helpful resource for lay people who are searching for a more coherent and compelling expression of Christianity."

—Mark Feldmeir, Senior Pastor, St. Andrew United Methodist Church, Highlands Ranch, Colorado

"In this book, Dr. Gould challenges Christianity to become the essence and soul of our civic and cultural well-being and to unite across its many fences that have divided us into separate religious camps for centuries. It is about what Christianity was meant to be. If you have given up on your faith's traditions or are no longer able to believe in its theological positions but are yearning to take a fresh look at faith, this is the book for you. It will lead you to a renewed understanding of God and a better relationship with your fellow human beings."

—Dan Nicholson, Retired Health Services Entrepreneur, Lino Lakes, Minnesota

"*An Open Christianity* is a book for persons who still seek to live authentic and true Christianity in the way and manner of Jesus in the twenty-first century dominated by science and technology, and an anti-science 'Christian nationalism' that attempts to control, dominate, and rule all of religious belief and practice. The book seeks to give a fresh, new life into an understanding of the term 'God' and what that means for persons of faith—with that built on a foundation of a deeper human comprehension and understanding of who Jesus really was and what he lived and taught and what he wanted human persons to be in concerned, compassionate connection to, with, for, and on behalf of others. Of course, what I've said here can only be comprehended and understood by reading the book and seeking to live the realities it details. This book will be a serious resource for those struggling with the faith of Christianity and old claims that no longer hold any significant meaning in the modern world. It will be a significant resource for pastors who want to be more open and honest about the issues of faith with the people they serve through their ministry. It is written and published at a time in history when it is needed more than ever for those seeking to live an authentic and true faith that Jesus lived and taught. The author of this book, Sam Gould, is an exceptional lay theologian who is deeply concerned with an authentic and true faith that can be lived in the modern world and is willing to share his deep concerns with others through his writing."

—Rodney Noel Saunders, Retired Clergy, United Methodist Church, Florissant, Colorado

An Open Christianity

An Open Christianity

SAM GOULD

WIPF & STOCK · Eugene, Oregon

AN OPEN CHRISTIANITY

Wipf & Stock
An Imprint of Wipf and Stock Publishers
199 W. 8th Ave., Suite 3
Eugene, OR 97401

www.wipfandstock.com

PAPERBACK ISBN: 979-8-3852-7216-7
HARDCOVER ISBN: 979-8-3852-7217-4
EBOOK ISBN: 979-8-3852-7218-1

VERSION NUMBER 02/10/26

For Elaine,

who has provided me with sustaining love for sixty-two years.

It is possible for people, and even for a whole society, to lose faith in God. . . . It happens, not primarily because they have decided that something they used to think existed does not after all exist, but because the available language about God has been allowed to become too narrow, stale and spiritually obsolete, and no longer functions as a satisfactory vehicle through which people can articulate their highest life-aims. The work of creative religious personalities is continually to enrich, to enlarge and sometimes purge the available stock of religious symbols and idioms so that faith in God shall continue to be possible. Certainly if faith in God is to flourish in a society as diverse and rapidly-changing as our own, then the more diverse religious thought becomes the better; whereas if on the other hand it is confined to a ghetto, closely policed and told to restrict itself to reiterating the idioms of the past, then faith in God will die. Unhappily, in many churches today that is exactly what is happening.

DON CUPITT, *THE SEA OF FAITH*

Contents

Acknowledgments

THIS BOOK WOULD NOT be possible had it not been for the late Rev. Walter Fitton, who, over fifty years ago, put me on a personal study of theology and contemporary religious thought. It is a debt for which I am forever grateful. Writing a book is a collaborative effort requiring patience and attention to detail, while not getting lost in one's own purpose. And that is where the help of others comes into the picture. While the matter of the content and style is my responsibility, the matters of clarity, sentence structure, and logic are shared responsibilities, and it is to many that I owe a debt of gratitude. First, my wife, Elaine, cheerfully read countless drafts of chapters, catching errors in grammar, logic, and judgment that has made the completion of this journey possible. The Rev. Rodney Saunders, retired Methodist clergy, helped me think through several of my theological positions and convey them more clearly. Of special note is his urging my expansion of Jesus's use of the "son of man" as a self-description. Likewise, a debt is owed to Dan Nicholson, who commented on every draft, made invaluable suggestions, and encouraged me to think more clearly about big picture items I was trying to communicate. A special thanks goes to Dr. Donald Lamm, who advised me on DNA and cellular science, reassuring me that I was not drifting away from accepted science. I also wish to thank Dr. Charles Wells, who read an early version of the manuscript, challenging the logic of several of my early assumptions. I also wish to thank Dr. Larry Rasmussen for sending me in the direction of framing the book as an eighty-year journey. I am also indebted to Rev. Dr. Steve Burnett, Rev. Mark Feldmeir, and Rev. Dr. Don Messer for reviewing, commenting, and supporting my work. I must also express my appreciation for the editors of Wipf and Stock Publishers for choosing to publish this book and all its efforts in bringing it successfully into print. In the end, the responsibility for the content and direction of this book lies solidly on my shoulders. But, without the keen attention of all of those mentioned, this volume would be lacking.

Introduction

CHRISTIANITY IS IN TROUBLE. The trouble didn't materialize overnight. Several geopolitical, technological, and societal events came together to form a perfect storm. A faith with which over 90 percent of American adults once identified had, by 2021, declined to 63 percent.[1] While the exodus has slowed, damage has already occurred, and there is no evidence that the decline will not accelerate again. Further, the politicization of the Christian right by one of the major political parties beginning in the 1970s has fueled a resurgence of the old and ugly movement of Christian nationalism. The great faith of love and charity is now morphing into a vehicle for spreading division and hate. This is hardly the intent of the Christian founders.

Unfortunately, Christianity itself has contributed to the decline. Beginning with the fundamentalist movement early in the last century, Christianity has evolved into a religion of belief in unviable outdated doctrines, dogmas, creeds, and theories. There have been warnings that have literally been ignored. As early as a century ago, Pierre Teilhard de Chardin warned of the need to modernize and update Christology. Literalism, a hallmark of fundamentalism, has created a dualism between believers and nonbelievers, setting up an artificial division among Americans, creating an opportunity to be exploited by savvy self-promoting politicians. Perhaps, as Harvey Cox has observed, it is time for the age of belief to be ushered out and the age of faith ushered in.[2] That is what this book is about.

1. Cox, *Future of Faith*, 19.
2. Cox, *Future of Faith*, 19.

What can be done about this situation Christianity now faces? Two centuries of theories, doctrines, and creeds have made faith largely unintelligible. Confusion exists over the nature of God and unbelievable stories of Jesus's short life challenge the modern intellect. Years of warning by theologians have remained largely a discussion between academic colleagues and not filtered down to the denominations, churches, and cults. Meanwhile, for most of the twentieth century, churches were artificially buoyed by supplementary forces unrelated to the faith itself. Unfortunately, since the 1990s, the church has failed to successfully respond.

This book is about a Christian journey. It's not about the journey itself but where the journey has led after eight decades of being a Christian. Those decades included years in Lutheranism, with its faith vs. works and creedal statements; in Presbyterianism, with its emphasis on God's sovereignty and governmental structure; with Methodism and its practical challenge to do no harm but all the good you can and its quadrilateral guide for understanding Scripture; with the Southern Baptists and their absence of creedal statements but emphasis on biblical literalism; and with Congregationalism and its liberalism and emphasis on action. The journey includes fifty years in various lay administrative and teaching positions in these churches and twenty years as a senior academic administrator at a Roman Catholic university.

After reading Dietrich Bonhoeffer's *Letters from Prison* and *Cost of Discipleship* in my early thirties, I began a multi-decade habit of reading religious authors with such diversity of thought as Tillich and Kaufman to Borg and Crossan; from Schillebeeckx, Kung, and Kierkegaard to Gutierrez, Spong, and Wink; from Teilhard de Chardin, Cox, and Delwin Brown to McLaren, Rohr, and Robin Meyers. While all of this may seem exhausting, the point is that this journey has encompassed a broad sampling of Christian writings, teachings, and practices. It is with this foundation, unbridled by academic convention and clerical limitations, that I propose an open Christianity that steers clear of preposterous claims and transactional incentives while reconstructing a faith one can truly believe.

The book is in three parts. "Part 1: Preliminary Matters" consists of the first two chapters, addressing the need for Christian reform and a brief introduction to an open Christianity. Chapter 1 is entitled "Christianity: A Religion on the Ropes." It chronicles the decline in the number of people identifying as Christian, identifies who are most likely to drop out, why they are leaving, and societal factors aiding the slide. It is noted that Christianity undergoes reform and renewal every five hundred years or so and suggests it is undergoing such a process currently.

For nearly a millennium and a half, from the time of the Roman initiative to make Christianity a national religion to the rise of Protestantism in the sixteenth century, the church spoke with a uniform voice. Martin Luther's rebellion birthed centuries of formation and then splintering of various Christian denominations, churches, and cults, creating an expression for people with differing needs, belief propensities, and aspirations. Our modern economy appreciates a "different strokes for different folks" strategy. A quick visit to the grocery store or pharmacy, with their variety of products to satisfy the appetite or a current ailment, will quickly convince anyone of this fact. But has this been beneficial for Christianity? Clearly, the Catholic church overplayed its hand with the selling of indulgences to finance the construction of St. Peter's, becoming the tipping point for rebellion. But the fragmentation of the church has also had the unanticipated result of creating independent Christian entities, each with their own version of Christianity, complete with their own theological emphasis and individual practices. Those theologies and practices are now protected within closed system walls, keeping them from being diluted and refuted. Survival became the ultimate concern for ensuring each brand's viability. The result is that Jesus's message, in many cases, has taken on a secondary importance.

Chapter 2 is entitled "An Open Christianity." The term was inspired by Jim Burklo's book *Open Christianity: Home by Another Road.*[3] Burklo's book follows a deconstructionist theme that has also been picked up by other authors in recent years. While many

3. Burklo, *Open Christianity.*

deconstructionists give permission to abandon doctrine, dogma, and creeds, they typically don't provide a reconstruction that can provide a foundation for vibrant faith. This chapter looks at today's structure of Christianity following a systems approach. Utilizing the thinking of sociology professor Amati Etzioni, Christian involvement is distinguished from a Christian commitment, the former, which is transactional in nature, and the latter, which is values-driven and leads to a transformational and transcendent faith of action. Drawing on the work of Howard Thurman, distinctions are made between treating Jesus as an object to be manipulated for one's own good or as a subject to learn from and emulate. The chapter ends with a discussion of how an open Christianity would differ from much of traditional Christianity.

"Part 2: Theological Matters" contains chapters 3 through 6, which address foundational concepts about God, Jesus, the human being, and the relationship between them.

Mark Feldmeir, in his book *Life After God*, describes the mess we have made of making assertions about God.[4] He simply admits that Christianity has a "God problem." Confusion reigns. Does God seek vengeance on non-believers? Did God require the brutal sacrifice of his only son to be reconciled with humanity? Does God control everything, actualizing an immutable plan in which we all play some role? Are "acts of God" really acts of God? Is God *love* as 1 John contends? Can God be all these things? If God is all these things, is this a deity that you can worship and model your life after? Or are many of these attributes simply human projection?

Chapter 3 is entitled "God." It begins drawing an analogy between God's spirit and the theme of Bruce Johnson's song "I Write the Songs," made popular by Barry Manilow. The point is made that God is beyond description, and so, we construct our gods to address matters that are beyond the boundaries of our personal agency. Hence the earliest images of YHWH were a war god and a storm god, addressing the two existential concerns that threatened the early nomadic Hebrews. Our concepts of God should become ever more sophisticated as we become more sophisticated. That

4. Feldmeir, *Life After God*.

is why our concept of God should not be trapped in the medieval mindset through which it is so frequently portrayed.

A 2006 Baylor study found four basic images that people have of God, meaning that there is no agreed upon understanding of the deity.[5] But if we pursue John's contention that God is love and compare it to Paul's description of love in 1 Cor, many of today's ideas and beliefs about God become questionable. To further flesh out an understanding of God, creation is described as a web of consciousness and God as the source of that unifying consciousness. From that basis, the chapter closes with a minimalist unifying metaphor proposed for God.

Jesus was born about the year 4 BCE. Legend has him born in Bethlehem. Perhaps, it was there, or perhaps, it was more likely his hometown of Nazareth. Nonetheless, narratives about him are bountiful. In some cases, they stretch the imagination beyond the breaking point. Is the Jesus portrayed in the Gospels to be taken literally? Did Jesus have his own objections to the use of supernatural powers? All good questions that are pursued in chapter 4.

Chapter 4 is entitled "Jesus." The information we have about this man was written by his admirers and is chronicled in the four Gospels. We can assume the narratives are biased, but within the bias, when placed in the context of the time, certain things can be deduced about the real Jesus. For example, the matter of crucifixion created a really difficult hole for the Jesus movement to climb out of. Crucifixion was beyond brutal, but it was also a means of execution that had broad public support in its day. How could a representative, perhaps even the very son of God, have his life end in such disgrace?

Another perplexing matter is why the Gospels have so many of Jesus's acts mimicking the acts of Moses. Was there an agenda his followers were pursuing after his death? Further, was some of the writing regarding supernatural events common assertions made about important people of the day? Would Jesus likely approve of the supernaturalism imposed upon him by his chroniclers? Would

5. Bader et al., "American Piety."

his time in the wilderness suggest otherwise? Did the wilderness experience open a window into the person Jesus chose to become?

Jesus was perhaps the first to choose what has become known as the servant leadership model, rejecting supernaturalism and political messiahship, but what is Jesus's self-description as "son of man" all about? Where did it likely come from and what does it suggest about Jesus's divinity? How did the Garden of Gethsemane experience validate the perfection of Jesus's humanity? The chapter culminates offering a minimalist statement for an open Christian understanding of Jesus.

Turning next to the human being, where does the human being fit into existence? What does it mean to be human and how are we to relate to fellow travelers in this great web of consciousness we know as reality? Are we uniquely human, or are we made of spare parts perfected centuries and millennia earlier by other beings? How should we relate to the mutually interdependent biosphere, whose existence we depend upon moment by moment for our very lives?

Chapter 5 is titled "The Human Being." How are we to responsibly fit into God's vast sea of consciousness? Being human starts with one's survival being heavily dependent on others, normally one's parents. In aging, greater independence is gained and a unique self begins to come into being. The existential questions of who I am and who I should become are paramount. When the self's outward projection aligns with the inner self understanding, a person is on the path to authenticity and integrity. But the human being is not self-sufficient or, indeed, an independent agent. Rather, it shares an evolutionary history and commonality with all sentient beings. The very life of the human is dependent on a vast existence of microbes, shared DNA, and processes common to all flora and fauna. Therefore, understanding the role of humans in sharing and preserving the vast ecology in which they live, breathe, and exist is crucial.

Chapter 6 is entitled "Source, Prototype, Work in Progress." The title reflects God as the source of all existence, exhibiting what being fully human means, Jesus as the prototype for God's full humanness expressed in flesh and blood, and us as beings at a stage of development short of full humanity. Jesus as our role model is briefly addressed, and then the leap is taken from self to transcendence of self for the common good. The mandates of proactive engagement in society, moral behavior, and ethical critique are distinguished. Guidance from Scripture is suggested as a means of assessing the motivation for both moral and ethical behavior. The chapter ends identifying two existential tasks of the open Christian.

"Part 3: Practical Matters" pivots to the current challenge of Christian Nationalism and how an open Christian fellowship or church might be formed.

Chapter 7 is entitled "Open Christianity and Christian Nationalism." Christian Nationalism is making another run at a comeback. It is a corruption of Christianity that many committed Christians easily fall prey to. What could go wrong with being a Christian nation? The first attempt at this in history occurred when Christianity became the official religion of the Roman Empire. It resulted in Romans no longer persecuting Christians but, rather, in Christians killing unorthodox Christians. With today's fragmentation of Christianity into thousands of denominations, churches, and cults, each maintaining and protecting their own beliefs and practices, one of them becoming the *official* Christianity would not end happily. Centuries of subverted church power validates this. In addition, the shallowest of examinations will show that those advocating Christian nationalism have beliefs and promote behaviors that, in no stretch of the imagination, could be called Christian. Chapter 7 briefly recounts the background of Christian nationalism, including its origins, current form, and recent research regarding the beliefs of its followers. The movement is critiqued from an open Christian perspective.

Chapter 8, "Advancing an Open Christian Expression," begins with drawing a parallel between Jesus's attempt to reform first-century Judaism's legalism and tradition of the elders with an open Christianity's eschewing of ancient doctrine, dogma, and creeds that so many find no longer believable. The chapter, drawing on

Jesus's warning about putting new wine in old wineskins, warns about the dangers of introducing church reforms. The experience of the United Methodists and other denominations are examples of what can go wrong. The chapter continues with expressions of an open Christianity for an individual and for a fellowship within a congregation. Open Christian perspectives are reviewed and an example of vision, mission, and initiatives of an open Christian church follow. The chapter ends with a reminder of the precarious condition traditional Christianity faces and expressing the hope that new thinking and new wine may reinvigorate what, in chapter 1, is called *a religion on the ropes.*

With that as an introduction, let's begin a journey into an open Christianity!

Sam Gould
Divide, Colorado
December 2025

PART 1

Preliminary Matters

1

Christianity: A Religion on the Ropes

The importance of the preservation of the inheritance from the past cultivates an attitude of caution and inclines an ancient organization to defend the status quo, to stand sponsor for outgrown customs, and to protect forms of worship and systems of thought which have become inadequate for the expanding life of the race.

RUFUS JONES

WHILE THE PERCENTAGE OF the population identifying as Christian has been in decline since the early 1990s and accelerated in the decade following 2007, the most recent Pew Religious Landscape study reports that the decline, at least for the moment, has stabilized.[1] This may give pause for taking a deep breath and assuming the worst is over. But that deep breath and sigh of relief may be premature. The pause is likely to be a temporary respite in the decline, since Christian disaffiliation is greatest among younger generations. It does not take a sophisticated survey and polling expertise to reach this conclusion. All one must do is attend a church service on any Sunday other than Christmas or Easter, and one

1. Pew Research Center, "Decline of Christianity."

will see a half-empty church filled with gray-haired congregants. Of course, there have been exceptions. For several years, evangelical churches seemed to be immune to this decline. It was the liberal and mainline congregations that were taking the hit. But a recent Public Religion Research Institute (PRRI) study reported that White evangelicals have dropped from 23 percent of adult Americans in 2006 to 13.6 percent in 2023.[2] Diana Butler Bass, in her book *Christianity After Religion*, wrote, "The belief that liberal churches fail while conservative ones prosper is no longer true. Everyone she says is in the same sinking boat."[3] She has coined the term "The Great Religious Recession" to describe the first decades of the twenty-first century. The question on many people's minds is, "Will there be a Great Religious Recovery?" The answer is, without substantially addressing the reasons people are leaving, probably not! In this chapter, we will report the extent and speed of the decline in those no longer identifying as Christian, look at the primary reason that people give for leaving Christianity, consider societal factors that artificially propped up Christianity in the past, and identify changes that have abetted its present decline. Based on these observations, a case will be made for a Christian reformation, for a more open Christianity.

THE DECLINE IN PEOPLE IDENTIFYING AS CHRISTIAN

The General Social Survey[4] in 1972 found that 93 percent of American adults identified as being Christian, and this held until the early 1990s. But today, people are leaving churches and dropping their Christian identity at a remarkable rate. Pew Religious Landscape studies report that, by 2007, the number of American adults identifying as Christian had dropped to 78 percent, and by

2. PRRI, "PRRI Census of American Religion."

3. Bass, *Christianity After Religion*, 18.

4. The General Social Survey (GSS) is a biennial, nationally representative survey of American adults, conducted by NORC at the University of Chicago beginning in 1972. Hout and Smith, "Fewer Americans Affiliate."

2021, it further declined to 63 percent. During the same period, the percentage identifying with no religion, referred to as "nones," grew from 16 percent to 29 percent. The "nones" consist of three groups: about 17 percent consider themselves atheists, 20 percent agnostics, and the largest group, 63 percent, report being "nothing in particular."[5]

This increase in disaffiliation has hit the Protestant churches most intensely. In 2021, Pew reported a decline in the American adult population identifying as Protestant from 52 percent in 2007 to 40 percent in 2021. The decline in this period for Catholics was a more moderate 24 percent to 21 percent. The proportion of adults identifying with non-Christian religions remained stable at 5 percent to 6 percent.[6]

Other reported measures of decline over the period from the 2021 report were the number reporting praying daily dropping from 58 percent of the population to 45 percent, while those reporting seldom or never praying grew from 18 percent to 32 percent of adults. Those reporting religion being "very important" in their lives dropped from 56 percent to 41 percent, while those reporting religion being "not too important" or "not at all important" more than doubled, rising from 16 percent to 33 percent.[7] This is clearly not a healthy scenario for the future of this once seemingly invincible western religion. But on an encouraging note, recently, PRRI reported that the percentage of nonaffiliated American adults hit a high point of 26 percent in 2018; by 2020, the percentage decreased to 23 percent.[8] Further, that turnaround came about primarily in mainline protestant congregations. As noted, a recent Pew Survey[9] reports that the decline in those identifying as Christian may have stabilized in the short term. It is unclear if this is an artifact of the recent COVID pandemic or some other dynamic. But we do know that much damage has already

5. Pew Research Center, "Decline of Christianity."
6. Pew Research Center, "About Three-in-Ten U.S. Adults."
7. Pew Research Center, "About Three-in-Ten U.S. Adults."
8. PRRI, "American Religious Landscape in 2020."
9. Pew Research Center, "Decline of Christianity."

been done, and many of the conditions that kept participation in Christianity artificially high in the past no longer exist.

WHO ARE MOST LIKELY TO DROP CHURCH AFFILIATION

The exit from Christianity is greatest among younger cohorts of the US population. The Pew Religious Landscape studies of 2007, 2014, and 2023–2024 provide snapshots of Christian identification over time, providing some insight into the disaffiliation dynamic. The data indicates that Christian affiliation remained stable at around 80 percent for American adults sixty-five and older. For those in the fifty to sixty-four-year-old cohort, the drop in affiliation was 9 percent over the period from 2007 to 2023–2024. The drop for younger cohorts was steeper. The cohort ages thirty to forty-nine saw a drop from 78 percent in 2007 to 54 percent in 2023–2024; and for the eighteen to twenty-nine-year-old cohort, the drop was from 68 percent identifying as Christian to 45 percent.[10] This might not be so alarming if the common understanding that people become more religious as they age were true. But the Pew longitudinal studies indicate that this is not true. People who disaffiliate early tend to stay disaffiliated. Further, the "stickiness" of religious fervor does not seem to pass on to the next generation. Adults brought up in highly religious families frequently do not tend to themselves be highly religious, and children of disaffiliated parents are unlikely, later in life, to become affiliated with Christianity.[11]

A Pew study in September 2022 estimates that between the ages of fifteen and twenty-nine, 31 percent of people raised as Christians disaffiliate and become "nones." It has also been estimated that twenty-six to forty-two million people raised in Christian homes will disaffiliate by 2050. There is some offset to this, as 21 percent of those under age thirty, who were raised with

10. Pew Research Center, "Religious Landscape Study."

11. Pew Research Center, "Decline of Christianity."

no religious affiliation, will convert to Christianity.[12] But this is a minor and inconsequential offset to the trend in disaffiliation that has been underway in the last few decades. In his book *The Making of Ex-Christian America*, Stephen Bullivant has coined the term "nonverts" for the two thirds of "nones" who grew up Christian but then converted to become unaffiliated.[13] If this trend continues at a similar pace, and as more children grow up in nonreligious families, the decline in Christianity will accelerate. Thus, while the precipitous decline in Christian affiliation has seen a leveling off, underlying dynamics suggest it is only a temporary reprieve.

WHY NONES ARE LEAVING CHRISTIANITY

According to a 2018 Pew survey, 67 percent of nones report they left Christianity because they no longer believe in God and/or no longer find Christian teaching believable. Only 13 percent of nones believe in God as described in the Bible, despite 59 percent reporting belief in "a higher power" other than the God of the Bible. Only 29 percent do not believe either in the God of the Bible or a higher power. However, belief in God is not only a problem with the nones. It also drops precipitously among those that have not disaffiliated but infrequently attend religious services. While 90 percent of nones seldom or never attend religious services, only 60 percent of those still identifying as Christian attend religious services monthly or less, with 46 percent attending seldom or never.[14] According to a 2023 Gallup survey, 98 percent of religiously affiliated people attending services weekly believe in God. However, among those attending religious services infrequently, belief in God drops to 57 percent. Overall, belief in God has dropped from 90 percent of American adults in 2001 to 74 percent in 2023. Belief in God also differed by age in the Gallup study. For those over the age of fifty-five, 83 percent believed in God. It dropped to

12. Pew Research Center, "Modeling the Future of Religion."
13. Bullivant, *Making of Ex-Christian America*.
14. Pew Research Center, "Why America's 'Nones' Don't Identify."

73 percent for those aged thirty-five to fifty-four, and 59 percent for those aged eighteen to thirty-four.[15] A fair conclusion is that God is portrayed in our contemporary religious organizations in a way that has lost credibility among the religiously unaffiliated as well as many still identifying as Christian.

Religious teaching about heaven and hell is also becoming dubious for many. According to the Gallup survey, over the period of 2001 to 2023, belief in heaven has dropped from 83 percent of the population to 67 percent, and belief in hell dropped from 71 percent to 59 percent.[16] Recent books in the marketplace are tapping into this dissatisfaction with orthodoxy and traditional teachings. Mark Feldmeir, in his book *Life After God*, wrote about faith after one can no longer *believe*.[17] Belden Lane, in his *Backpacking with the Saints*, writes of his spiritual experiences during seclusion in the wilderness.[18] John Robinson, in *I Am God*, presents poetry aimed at experiencing the very consciousness of God that is accessible within oneself.[19] Jan Linn, in *Unbinding Christianity*, wrote about a values vs. belief-based faith.[20] Oord and Fuller, in their book *God After Deconstruction*, discussed deconstruction of religious belief and reconstructing a faith that one can believe.[21] A common theme in these and other writings distinguishes between beliefs that are to be taken as fact and a faith that touches the very identity, the very soul of a person. Clearly, these authors' works demonstrate that there is movement by many away from belief in traditional Christian teachings and orthodoxy.

15. Brenen, "Belief in Five Spiritual Entities."
16. Brenen, "Belief in Five Spiritual Entities."
17. Feldmeir, *Life After God.*
18. Lane, *Backpacking with the Saints.*
19. Robinson, *I Am God.*
20. Linn, *Unbinding Christianity.*
21. Oord and Fuller, *God After Deconstruction.*

SOCIETAL FACTORS AIDING DISAFFILIATION

As belief in religious teaching wanes among a significant portion of the population, several societal factors are effective catalysts for the phenomenon of disaffiliation and low church attendance among Christians. One of these factors is the Republican Party's politicization of the Christian Right, i.e., conservative evangelical and fundamentalist Christians, who strongly oppose social and cultural trends supporting abortion, gay rights, non-binary genders and related matters, intensifying the potential for a polarized electorate. The GOP's identification with the Christian Right hit its high during the presidency of George W. Bush, who claimed to be one of their own and spoke the evangelical language. More recently, the Trump MAGA movement has tapped into the Christian Right sector to win the power of the presidency in 2016 and again in 2024. During George W. Bush's presidency, White evangelicals were the largest religious group in the country. But as we have noted, White evangelicals have recently also experienced decline. Some of these deserters have joined mainline congregations, but many have just left the Christian fold, all because their political views were no longer compatible with their church's positions. It seems too obvious to have to state this, but as soon as you align yourself with a political party, you lose the commitment of those who identify with another party or no party at all. Politicians aligning with a Christian sector may bolster a candidate's chances of winning an election, but it has a deleterious effect on Christianity, creating disenchantment within another Christian sector, accelerating disaffiliation.

Differing theological views on LGBTQ+ issues have been a dividing issue for many Christians, and not just for the Christian Right. Mainline churches have splintered over this issue. Congregants within denominations have differed over acceptance of same-sex marriage and ordaining LGBTQ+ clergy. This has divided and imperiled Presbyterian, United Church of Christ, Episcopal, Baptist, and Mennonite congregations over the past decades. The latest denomination to split over the issue is the United Methodist

Church. This has had two damaging effects on Christianity. First, it divides Christians into three camps: those in the accepting camp, those in the rejecting camp, and those who just become disgusted, throw up their hands, and disaffiliate, thus accelerating Christianity's decline.

But there is an additional peril with this matter and perhaps the most alarming one for Christianity's future. A recent Gallup poll found that those not just sympathetic toward LGBTQ+ inclusion but identifying as LGBTQ+ has grown to 9.3 percent of the adult population.[22] And even more startling, according to the survey, 23 percent of those born from 1997 to 2006 and 14 percent born from 1981 to 1996 identify as LGBTQ+.[23] The percentage of those identifying as LGBTQ+ then declines precipitously with the older cohorts. The question is, if this trend continues, who is going to replace the conservative gray-haired members of congregations when they die, and the entire population becomes more accepting of LGBTQ+ individuals and couples? Perhaps no one.

Bullivant points to the end of the Cold War as a triggering point in the decline of Christian affiliation, perhaps the initial one.[24] The Cold War ended in 1991 with the collapse of the Soviet Union. During the height of the Cold War, the religious West was pitted against the atheist Soviet Bloc. This had the effect of closely associating Christianity with American patriotism, giving Christianity an artificial buoyancy. While many people may have previously had a lukewarm commitment to their religious tradition, they nonetheless found it awkward and unpopular not to identify as Christian. Jim Davis and Michael Graham, in their book *The Great Dechurching*, wrote that during the Cold War, the terms "American" and "Christian" were often used interchangeably in the struggle against a foreign nation that posed a grave threat to the American way of life.[25] Contrast that to today, when many of the issues that the Christian Right condemns (abortion, gay rights,

22. Jones, "LGBTQ+ Identification in U.S."

23. Jones, "LGBTQ+ Identification in U.S."

24. Bullivant, *Nonverts*, 124.

25. Davis and Graham, *Great Dechurching*, 4–5.

gender identity, etc.) are also condemned by the Orthodox church in Putin's Russia. Thus, the bond between religious affiliation and patriotism has been muddied, reducing the societal pressure to religiously affiliate.

A second factor that Bullivant cites is the rise of the internet and social media.[26] Prior to this phenomenon, many people with divergent religious views were isolated and social pressure kept them from openly expressing their opinions. Many people living in small towns could go their entire lives without ever knowing an atheist. But now, people with unfavorable views of Christianity can find like-minded people on the internet, reinforcing and supporting their opinions. Indeed, an embarrassment of riches in anti-Christian support can be found on the internet to reinforce and mold a person's anti-Christian inclinations. Local community social pressure has lost much of its dominance.

But social media and the internet have not had only a negative impact on religion. Beginning with the COVID pandemic, it has also impacted Christianity and, indeed, all world religions in a positive way. Influencers on TikTok, Instagram, YouTube, and elsewhere have led sessions supporting and explaining the elements of Christian faith in a positive format. A Pew survey report in 2022 found the nearly 50 percent of American adults are at least light users of online religious media, and 26 percent are moderate to heavy users.[27] Recent experience has shown this to be a path to faith for those with little interest in traditional Sunday church services.

But even this has a downside. Christian advocates are often derided and ridiculed online. Further, sites are also dedicated to tearing down and ridiculing Christianity. New forms of Christian belief are being proposed, some with legitimate scriptural support, others without adequate underpinning. In too many cases, the popularity of a site is based on charismatic appeal rather than on legitimate competence in Christian thought and theology. Many of these sites worldwide receive billions of hits or views, and they,

26. Bullivant, *Nonverts*, 121.

27. Pew Research Center, "Online Religious Services Appeal."

too, often distort Christianity rather than purport a legitimate theology. As with all technological advances, they may have a positive or a negative impact. Most recently, they have had a negative impact.

Bullivant also attributes the rise of the "nones" and "nonverts" to it being "trendy" and, therefore, enduring less social criticism from peers and neighbors.[28] As their numbers grow, it is easier for "nones" and "nonverts" to find fellow travelers in their local social networks. Strangely enough, Bullivant himself grew up in a nonreligious family and converted to Catholicism at age thirty-eight.[29] Unfortunately, this is a rare phenomenon. For everyone like him, there are twenty-six people going in the other direction.

IT IS TIME TO RETHINK CHRISTIANITY

Several dynamics have been creating an uphill battle for Christianity's vibrancy in the past three decades. They include the end of the Cold War, which had previously aligned Christianity with American patriotism and the rise of the internet and social media, which then diminished the influence of relative social isolation and provided reinforcement of anti-Christian attitudes from broader social networks. We have seen how progressive social attitudes have strengthened; their seeds being sown in the 1960s civil rights and women's liberation movements. These movements toward greater social tolerance recently include not just gender equality but also same-sex marriage and gender diversity. This threatens traditionalists who yearn for the past. But the truth is that the genie cannot be put back in the bottle. Societal tolerance is most likely to continue expanding, and perhaps at an accelerated pace. These social movements, in many people's eyes, are counter to traditional Christian teaching. Further, there seems to be very little conservative Christianity can do to stop this avalanche from happening. As threatening as this all may seem, Christianity is not

28. Bullivant, *Nonverts*.

29. Bullivant, *Nonverts*.

defenseless. The things that are in its wheelhouse can control how Christianity communicates God, interpretates Scripture, and talks about the role of Jesus.

Since the Council of Nicaea in the early fourth century CE, the Christian intelligentsia has wrestled with what one must *believe* to be Christian. These beliefs have found their way into today's body of doctrine, dogma, and creeds. This process has often not led to good outcomes. Establishing an orthodoxy or right belief, then thrusting it upon the Christian family has separated Christians from the richness that other world religions could provide. But unfortunately, that is the lesser issue. Orthodoxy has resulted in even more egregious outcomes, evidenced by untold atrocities and blood being spilt across world religion boundaries. And this divisiveness has not stopped there. It also has occurred within the Christian family, when orthodoxy has been invoked to divide and subdue aberrant thinking and consolidate power in clerical ranks. In the extreme, it has led to justifying Christians killing Christians. In lesser extremes, it has led to divisiveness and disunity within the Christian family. All of this is contradictory to Jesus's project of *the kingdom*, encompassing love of God and love of neighbor as its essence.

Christian orthodoxy, created in a time of scientific innocence and societal/cultural structures, long since reformed and transformed, has led to today's dilemma. Standard orthodoxy is increasingly difficult for many good-hearted souls to believe. Hence, we have the exodus from Christianity that we are now experiencing. Among those still identifying as Christians, deconstruction, the jettisoning of beliefs that no longer seem plausible, is a growing trend. But is deconstruction a satisfactory solution to stop or slow Christianity's slide into obscurity? What does deconstruction leave behind? Can it be a faith that is inspiring, soul-grabbing, and sustainable? Or will it likely to lead to a patchwork faith, lukewarm and inspiring only more irregularity in Christian service attendance?

Reforming and restating Christian beliefs are not new ideas. As early as a century ago, Pierre Teilhard de Chardin argued that we need to restate our Christology—that in its current state, it is no longer intelligible to moderns.[30] Paul Tillich has argued for a reinterpretation of God, from a being to the ground of being, and not found up there or out there somewhere but found in our very depth.[31] Mark Feldmeir has more recently argued that God is the elephant in the room that we never fully discuss but all assume everyone knows about.[32] It is as though we have attached so many claims to the word God that the whole concept has become untenable. Don Cupitt argues that "the available language about God has been allowed to become too narrow, stale, and spiritually obsolete, and no longer functions as a satisfactory vehicle through which people can articulate their highest life–aims."[33] He continues, if faith in God "is confined to a ghetto, closely policed and told to restrict itself to reiterating the idioms of the past, then faith in God will die."[34]

Perhaps the whole idea of basing Christianity on a system of beliefs is wrongheaded. Since the greatest Christian commandments are to love God and neighbor, outcomes and process, not belief, is what matters in the end. Some think we are already in a period of reform and moving in that direction. Phyllis Tickle, in *The Great Emergence*, wrote that Christianity undergoes revision and reform about every five hundred years. Further, she believed we are now in such a transition.[35] Harvard theologian Harvey Cox also sees significant change ahead. In *The Future of Faith*, Cox argues that we are in the process of transitioning from an age of belief to an age of faith and spirit.[36] Diana Butler Bass, in her book *Christianity After Religion*, writes that we are in a period of a new spiritual awakening.[37]

30. Teilhard de Chardin, *Christianity and Evolution.*
31. Tillich, *Courage to Be.*
32. Feldmeir, *Life After God*, 17.
33. Cupitt, *Sea of Faith*, 249–50.
34. Cupitt, *Sea of Faith*, 249–50.
35. Tickle, *Great Emergence.*
36. Cox, *Future of Faith.*
37. Bass, *Christianity After Religion.*

While some may think progressive social change poses an insurmountable threat to Christianity and that reform and restructuring signal the end of Christianity, it may actually open new vistas and possibilities for Christian faith and for enriching and deeply touching our lives in new and exciting ways. But such change must preserve the richness of Christianity's foundational message, encompassing the whole person, both head and heart. I believe a reformed Christianity can empower our yearning for transcendence, creating a world more aligned with Jesus's vision of the kingdom, a world where unity, not division, prevails. A Christian reformation movement will challenge us to dig deeper into the essence of Christianity and how we might reinterpret it and preserve the faith for future generations. This must be an urgent priority for our churches. But it is not only for our churches; it is about us individually. As John F. Kennedy put it at the end of his 1961 inaugural address, "God's work must truly be our own."[38] And so, it must be.

Top-down theology and belief systems may have run their course. Since it is our souls and inner essence at stake, why should we, as individuals, exclusively entrust this matter to a religious industry, with its own agenda enforced by belief systems that are increasingly becoming irrelevant and unintelligible to moderns? Take responsibility back. This book offers an invitation to do so and a way to work out your own salvation in all seriousness, as Paul wrote, *with fear and trembling.*[39]

THOUGHT EXERCISES

1. What are your thoughts regarding the declining percentage of people identifying as Christian? Have you seen this in your own congregation? Is this a serious threat to faith?
2. Do you agree with Bullivant that contributing factors to the rise of the "nones" are the internet and fall of the Soviet

38. Kennedy, "Inaugural Address," para. 28.

39. Phil 2:12.

Union? Had it occurred to you that patriotism was a reason people were hesitant to leave Christianity prior to the fall of the Soviet Union?

3. According to the Pew studies, many people no longer believe in traditional religious teachings. Why do you think this is the case? Have you questioned some of these teachings?
4. Are there religious teachings that you overlook, no longer recite, or interpret differently to stay Christian?
5. Do you believe Christianity is in a period of reform and re-thinking? If so, do you think this is a good thing or not?

2

An Open Christianity

The purpose of doctrine is not primarily to fill our heads but to shape our lives. We express our beliefs in words in order to express our beliefs in actions. The words are meant to promote deeds.

PAUL KNITTER

TODAY, FOR MANY, DOCTRINES have lost their power to inspire and shape lives, as Knitter suggests they should. And this has not happened overnight. We saw in the last chapter how calls for reform have been coming for decades. The disaffiliation we are experiencing is a warning sign that the status quo is no longer working. Many Christians not disaffiliating infrequently attend services and, in private, discard or deconstruct traditional Christian beliefs. These are all signs that reform is inevitable and, in many cases, is already underway. But what will reform look like? Could or should there be an organized approach to reform? Or must reform take many paths before it comes together, if that is even possible? In this chapter, we will consider an open Christianity as an approach to reform.

In 1975, fresh out of a PhD in program in organizational behavior, I began a thirty-year career in academe. I had not gone in a straight line directly from undergraduate studies into a PhD program. Rather, my high school sweetheart and I married just prior to my senior year in college. After graduation, my career began at a parts division of a large automobile manufacturer in Flint, Michigan. Before leaving, I had risen to an executive-level position as manager of data operations. But that was not a straight-line journey either. A few years earlier, I received a draft notice as the Vietnam conflict heated up. This was a few years before the draft lottery system was instituted. A draft notice meant that if you could pass a physical examination, you were headed to military service. I responded by volunteering for the Air Force Officer Training School, then at Lackland Air Force Base in San Antonio. After receiving a commission, beginning, and completing four years of active duty, earning an MBA degree along the way, my wife and I returned to corporate life in Michigan. But this time, with two little boys and, as the Air Force put it, one in the hangar. Our third son was born shortly thereafter. Children have the effect, at least for my wife and me, of thinking more deeply about the people and parents we wanted to be and the family life we wished to have. This led us not just back to graduate school and a career in academe but also to a life actively wrestling with the questions of what it means to be Christian. The wrestling continues and is an impetus for writing this book and thinking about what an open Christianity might be.

Organizational behavior is the study of how an enterprise can most effectively be structured to achieve its objectives. Structure pertains not only to macro issues, such as arranging the organizational units and establishing lines of authority, but also to establishing goals and objectives as well as the micro issues of incentive arrangements and management styles best suited for achieving the desired outcomes. An area I became intently interested in was how and why people become committed to organizations and movements. A natural progression was to apply this same discipline to my experience with Christianity.

Today, Christianity has literally become an unwieldy worldwide conglomeration of hundreds, if not thousands, of independent Christian denominations, churches, sects, and cults. Each has its own structure, beliefs, organization, and practices that differentiate it from other denominations, churches, sects, and cults. Some might think that this is a good thing, providing more choice for more people—different strokes for different folks, so to speak. But if, and it is a big "if," Christianity has or should have a common purpose, is there the potential for *mission* drift across these independent entities? And can the independent structures, beliefs, organizations, and practices take on an importance as great as Christianity's common purpose, or even supersede it? These are the questions we will consider next.

Perhaps, the best way to begin is with a brief bit of history. For centuries after Rome's blessing of Christianity, beginning in the early fourth century CE, Christianity was under the exclusive domain of the Catholic church. The church had unparalleled power to formulate the guardrails for defining how a Christian should act and what they must believe. Unfortunately, as Lord Acton warned, "Power corrupts, absolute power corrupts absolutely."[1] Early in the sixteenth century, the flagrant selling of indulgences caught the attention of Martin Luther, a priest and professor of theology at the University of Wittenberg. Proceeds from selling indulgences were used by the papacy to bolster funding for the construction of St. Peter's Basilica in Rome.[2] Purchasing an indulgence promised the purchaser forgiveness of sins they had already confessed and allegedly shortened their stay in purgatory.[3]

In the fall of 1517, Luther drafted ninety-five statements attacking the practice of selling indulgences and nailed them to the door of Wittenberg Castle Church and other area churches.[4] This was the beginning out of which grew Protestant Christianity.[5] What had been a unified, albeit exploitive church, now had

1. Dalberg, "Acton-Creighton Correspondence," para. 22.

2. Justice, "Role of Indulgences."

3. Purgatory is a Roman Catholic doctrine holding that, after death, even those escaping hell would likely spend time in a middle ground for the purifying of their soul prior to being permitted entry into heaven.

4. Luther, "Ninety-Five Theses."

5. October 31, the date in 1517 Luther is believed to have taken this action, is celebrated in many Protestant churches as Reformation Day.

a rival movement. That was just the beginning of Christianity's splintering. Grappling with expressing the inexpressible led to further splitting that ultimately led to today's proliferation of Christian expression and, along with it, a desire by each entity to perpetuate their own *brand*. With minor exceptions, these Christian entities talk freely within their cluster; they talk infrequently across liturgical boundaries. In effect, they act as closed systems infrequently exchanging information and ideas across rigid boundaries. As we shall see shortly, this organizational structure is prone to flaws, which limit its effectiveness and even distorts its very purpose and reason for being.

THE NATURE OF SYSTEMS

A system is an entity consisting of human and physical resources committed to providing some desired outcome while following a set of rules, beliefs, and procedures. Systems may be either tightly or loosely connected to form an overall superordinate system. Each system within a superordinate system constitutes its various subsystems, each contributing to the overall success or failure of the superordinate system. If we think of Christianity being the superordinate system, then each of the denominations, churches, sects, and cults are the subsystems that constitute it.

Systems, whether superordinate or subsystem components of the superordinate system, tend to be either open or closed. Briefly, open systems readily exchange information from outside their system boundaries and adapt to the best methods for optimizing their contribution to achieving the objective of the superordinate system. Closed systems are more inwardly focused and rarely exchange information beyond their system boundaries. They ignore or mute feedback that could signal a need to update practices to enhance their effectiveness. This often elevates maintaining often outdated internal methods and practices above the superordinate system's objective. Closed Christian systems operate like silos, protecting their innards from pollution and external contamination emanating from outside its impermeable walls. As such, they tend to be static, resistant to change, divisive, and cause the overall enterprise to perform suboptimally. Today's Christianity is a closed superordinate system composed of an unwieldy and loosely connected number of closed subsystems, each protecting their own turf. An open Christianity would follow an open system design, taking in information through porous boundary walls while seeking to optimize their members' contribution to Christianity's superordinate objective.

Open and Closed Systems

Information from environment bounces off impenetrable boundary

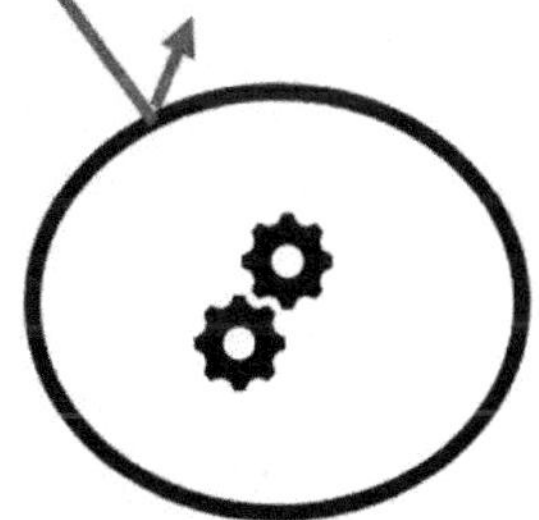

Information from environment penetrates porous boundary and the system adapts accordingly

PRACTICES, BELIEFS, AND OUTCOMES

Closed Christian entities, each with their preferred organization, missions, beliefs, and practices, easily fall prey to becoming inwardly focused, favoring self-preservation over Christianity's overarching goal. In such cases, form and belief take precedence over outcomes. The result is that Christianity itself becomes a confusing conglomeration of entities with often opposing objectives that have little to do with an ultimate Christian objective. This only muddies the waters and obscures what Christianity seeks to accomplish. Consider these differences among Christian systems. Some restrict Holy Communion only to church members in good standing while others practice an open table, where everyone is welcome. Some prohibit women from serving communion and assuming other roles and responsibilities in the church. Others ordain women to the ministry. Some regard nontraditional gender roles and sexual preferences as sinful; others accept these differences. Some churches proliferate a belief in the infallibility of Scripture or take Scripture literally, while others dig deeply into Scripture's often deeper meaning. Do any of the above restrictive matters advance an ultimate objective for Christianity? Do any of these differences between Christian practices advance the Christian mission? If so, I must wonder how they do so.

If this doesn't create enough diversion, there are also words and phrases that have questionable meaning. For example, "salvation" is a word ubiquitous to Christianity, but what does it mean? Is it personal or commutative? Does it mean saving people from going to hell after they die? Some churches seem to emphasize this. Does it mean saving someone from a life focused inwardly and primarily on pursuit of material objects? Does it mean building a social movement based on love of the other? Is the church to be a place of retreat and experiencing the sacred, or is it a place to undergird congregants with the love to cope in the greater reality? Is trusting in certain doctrines, dogma, creeds, and beliefs the goal of Christianity, or is it something more? Is Christianity meant to be a transactional relationship with the divine? Is it one where doing or believing certain things will gain one benefits in the present and eternal bliss in the hereafter? Or is Christianity a path to transcendence, where one's essence becomes saturated with love?

Another problem is the concreteness with which much of Christian thought is expressed. Knitter argues that Christianity expressing the mystery of God in concrete and precise language leaves one wondering, if it is not to be taken literally, then just how should it be taken?[6] Examples he gives are "three persons in God" and "Jesus sits at the right hand of the Father." Other examples might include "born of the virgin Mary" and "Jesus will come again to judge the quick and the dead." Perhaps, statements such as these

6. Knitter, *Without Buddha*, 57.

were enough in the past to convince people of the necessity of being Christian, even if they did not fully grasp their meaning. Today, they are not only less convincing but seem archaic and do little to bolster Christianity and produce fruitful Christian outcomes.

An open Christianity would subordinate organization, practice, and belief to the outcomes achieved by a Christian entity. An open Christianity would seek to clean up its language so that words designed to lead and guide people in the Christian faith do not become belief barriers and stumbling blocks themselves. In an open Christianity, the mystery we call God would more appropriately be described in mysticism, poetry, and metaphor as the *go to* forms of language. But left unresolved to this point in our discussion is the question, "What is the superordinate objective of Christianity that would determine if Christian initiatives were successful?" We shall turn to this next.

A SUPERORDINATE OBJECTIVE FOR AN OPEN CHRISTIANITY

As we have seen, Christianity does not speak with one tongue. Christian churches, denominations, and other Christian entities have their own emphases on what Christianity is all about. Some exist to save souls, others to spread the gospel, and still others to make disciple of Jesus. But does there need to be so many different objectives for the Christian movement? All of Christianity has its roots in the person of Jesus of Nazareth. Most simply, Jesus's life example and teachings are believed to accurately represent the intentions or hope of God for humanity. Jesus talked about a *kingdom*. His kingdom had no geographic boundaries as a political unit would. Rather, it was a system or cultural setting where the greatest commandments of loving God and neighbor were elevated above all else. Jesus's teachings and life example help us add concreteness to these abstract principles. I propose that the superordinate outcome for an open Christianity would simply be loving God and expressing that love by unconditionally loving all of God's creation, including one's neighbor, whether friend or foe.

CHRISTIAN ATTACHMENT: IDENTIFICATION OR COMMITMENT?

In this chapter, we have moved away from form and belief as the core of Christianity to consider instead the core being the outcomes Christianity fosters. In short, those outcomes being a society characterized by love of God and neighbor. In doing so, we will make a distinction between having a Christian identity and having a Christian commitment—the former being a transactional attachment, and the latter a path to transformative faith.

Amitai Etzioni, an Israeli American sociologist, passed away in June 2023 at age ninety-four. While at George Washington University in the 1990s, he became known as the father of the Communitarian movement, which advocated for a society in which people care for the common good rather than merely about themselves. Etzioni is the son of parents who fled to Palestine to evade Hitler's Holocaust. In 1957, he immigrated to the United States.[7] I came across Etzioni's work in 1975 when I was working on my dissertation at Michigan State University. It was Etzioni's work on organizational attachment that caught my attention.

Etzioni described three types of organizational attachment. Each is contingent on the type of power exercised to elicit it. Alienative attachment results when it is motivated by coercion, as when one is threatened with punishment for not behaving or believing appropriately. It is characterized by feelings of entrapment and hostility. A second type, calculative attachment, develops when one's involvement provides promise of receiving a valued outcome. Both alienative and calculative involvement are transactionally motivated, i.e., one's behavior is motivated by extrinsic factors, such as threats of punishment or promises of reward.[8] Either may lead to a positive or negative *identification* with Christianity.

Etzioni's third type is moral attachment. It occurs when one's attachment is fueled by an opportunity to exercise one's core values. This attachment is reinforced by self-derived internal rewards

7. McFadden, "Amitai Etzioni, 94, Dies."

8. Etzioni, *Comparative Analysis of Complex Organizations.*

attained simply from being involved. It is not dependent on an external threat of punishment or promise of reward. With moral attachment, the reward is intrinsic, independent, and internally motivated. It is the joy, well-being, or sense of satisfaction one experiences when they help someone in need or make a significant contribution to a worthy project. Moral attachment can be so powerful that an individual's behavior may appear selfless and counter to one's best interests. Moral attachment becomes more than identification with an entity; it becomes a commitment to it.[9]

One's relationship to Christianity can be described within this framework. For example, a heaven/hell theology offers threats and incentives that are inherent in alienative and calculative forms of attachment. These extrinsic motivators lie outside the individual and, by their very nature, are transactional. Transactional doctrines, offering punitive and/or positive incentives, are increasingly becoming a dead-end street as belief in God and many Christian teachings dwindle. A theology fostering moral attachment is transformational, captures the soul, and spawns a deep Christian commitment. It fosters a faith whose depth has no bottom.

JESUS, SUBJECT OR OBJECT?

Howard Thurman, in his book *Jesus and the Disinherited*, described an insight he had after being asked to explain why he was a Christian.[10] He said he felt challenged to write about Jesus as a religious subject rather than a religious object. Much of Christianity has treated Jesus as an object to be manipulated for one's own purpose in a transactional relationship that is undergirded by a belief matrix. This matrix forms the link between Jesus and both feared and desired outcomes. Conversely, Jesus as a *subject* opens us to learn from and possibly emulate his life and teaching. It is the pathway to transcendence, to becoming something more than we are. It is through this process we can experientially develop an

9. Etzioni, *Comparative Analysis of Complex Organizations.*

10. Thurman, *Jesus and the Disinherited.*

existential faith that grows deep within our *values* framework to fuel a committed faith journey.

Transactional exchanges carry limited personal emotive force. Lacking personal emotive force, a transactionally fueled Christianity frequently results in behaviors that don't seem very Christlike. Instead of doing the work involved in developing an existential values driven framework, using the shortcut of a belief matrix can become an irrational shortcut to defining one's Christian pilgrimage. Christianity, based on dubious transactional beliefs, can become, as John Robinson warns, a prison, controlling what you can experience and understand. Further, doubling down with even more beliefs will only make you less free.[11]

An existential values framework is self-reinforcing. Exercising one's values leads to what Paul called the "fruits of the spirit": "love, joy, peace, patience, kindness, generosity, faithfulness, gentleness, and self-control" (Gal 5:22). When behavior is inconsistent with one's values, one experiences an uncomfortable dissonance. Thus, behavior consistent with our deeply held values intrinsically empowers us, while inconsistent behavior is discomforting. A values-centered Christianity touches our essence, our soul. It creates within us a faith-based Christianity, which is distinguishable from a narrow belief-based Christianity. It is an *Open Christianity* that honors love above all and devalues any teachings, biblical or otherwise, that lack or diminish love. It is a Christianity focused on the greatest commandments endorsed by Jesus, in his supplemental teaching examples, and his lived story that embodied them. Internalization of and the pursuit of these values lacks the false certainty of a transactional belief system. In turn, it provides the depth for a committed Christian faith journey. Philosopher Alan Watts captured this when he distinguished between belief and faith-based religions in the following.

> Belief . . . is the insistence that the truth is what one would . . . wish it to be. The believer will open his mind to the truth on condition that it fits in with his own preconceived ideas and wishes. Faith on the other hand, is

11. Robinson, *I Am God*, 102.

> an unreserved opening of the mind to the truth, whatever it may turn out to be. Faith has no preconceptions; it is a plunge into the unknown. Belief clings, but faith lets go. In this sense of the word, faith is the essential virtue of science, and likewise of any religion that is not self-deception.[12]

AN OPEN CHRISTIANITY

An open Christianity is an open system. That means its ultimate focus is on achieving Christianity's superordinate objective, which it understands as Jesus's greatest commandment of loving God with all one's heart, mind, and strength and neighbor as oneself. It evaluates all interpretations of Scripture, creeds, doctrines, dogma, worship traditions, liturgies, and practices as to how they contribute to achieving this objective. An open Christianity is *outcomes*-oriented while minimizing dependence on belief structures, especially those that stretch the fabric of one's imagination. But to be clear, an open Christianity is not a neo-literal approach. Traditional teachings are set aside only after mining the deeper allegorical or metaphorical implications of the teaching. Further, those teachings with deeper meaning that seem suspect at the literal level are not to be separated from or presented without being accompanied by their deeper meaning. An open Christianity avoids supernatural explanation but instead looks to the *natural* as God's realm and gift to humankind. Theologies and doctrines are understood to be human endeavors to express the divine mystery, however imperfectly they may do so, and scientific endeavor is understood as an activity in partnership with God.

An open Christianity, as an open system, is an organic learning entity. It continually assesses its effectiveness in achieving its overall objective. It does not fear change or reject new methods or understandings because they challenge traditional practices and teachings. Further, an open Christianity invests in education. It

12. Watts, *Wisdom of Insecurity*, 24.

understands that to be effective in society, it must not only have both a basic understanding of Christian teaching but also have a means of practicing the essence of Christianity in the community.

An open Christianity, as an open system, engages with the greater reality within which it exists. It eschews the dualism between sacred and secular and understands the concept of Jesus's kingdom as the fruit that will be present when love of God and neighbor is manifest. Open Christian worship addresses the human condition and includes in worship not only traditional hymns, Scripture, and liturgies but also contemporary poetry, music, and stories that touch the heart and enrich the human journey. Further, an open Christianity does not avoid moral and ethical critique of social actions. It does not pass the buck to God to solve problems in society but sees God working in humankind to advance the kingdom.

An open Christianity is bottom-up. An open Christian entity may assist an individual to formulate a theology, but it is ultimately the individual's responsibility to do so. In a sense, an open Christianity's theology is personal and, therefore, contingent on an individual's personal needs, education, and experience. It is also open-ended, meaning that it develops and matures with time. But within an open Christian gathering, it is important for one's personal theology to remain open and shared.

Paul, in his own way, took a contingency approach to spreading the gospel, meeting the needs and experiences of those he was addressing. He wrote the following.

> To the Jews I became like a Jew. . . . To those under the law I became like one under the law. . . . To those not having the law I became like one not having the law, To the weak I became weak, to win the weak. I have become all things to all people so that by all possible means I might save some. I do all this for the sake of the gospel, that I may share in its blessings.[13]

13. 1 Cor 9:19–23.

Rejecting or challenging long-standing Christian doctrine or seeking a new understanding of the nature of Scripture may be difficult for many Christians. And many Christians are not well equipped to do this, having received or sought little Christian education after middle school or, at best, high school. The remainder of this book is designed to provide a starting point for building a personal and communal open Christianity that may serve them and the faith in years to come. To begin this journey, we will next address the matter of God. Through the centuries, our concept of God has become muddled with doctrine, dogma, theories, and theologies meant to enhance our understanding of God but have rather made our understanding of God not clearer—but indeed, more confounding. In chapter 3, we will work toward an understanding of God that can serve as a foundation for an open Christianity.

THOUGHT EXERCISES

1. Have you thought of the various motivations you have had or now have for being Christian? What has been your experience?
2. Is the distinction between Christian identity and Christian commitment a fruitful distinction to make for understanding one's faith involvement? Why do you think so or not think so?
3. Would placing emphasis on a values-based faith be better suited for the future of Christianity than emphasizing a belief-based faith? Why do you believe so or not believe so?
4. Are there Christian teachings you have difficulty believing? If so, what do you do about it?
5. Can you accept a wholistic world in which there is not a distinction between sacred and secular, between motivation driven by the head versus the heart? Please explain.
6. What are your thoughts regarding an open Christianity?

PART 2

Theological Matters

3

God

I've been alive forever, and I wrote the very first song
I put the words and the melodies together
I am music, and I write the songs.
Bruce Johnston

Music with pleasing vibrating rhythms can profoundly touch our consciousness. The above epigraph is from a song made famous by Barry Manilow in 1976. It was written by Bruce Johnston. The title of the song is "I Write the Songs." It was reported that Barry Manilow was reluctant to record the song, fearing people might think he was referring to himself as the "writer of songs" rather than it being a metaphor for God.[1] Perhaps, just as quantum physics holds that all of existence consists of energy and vibrational frequency, it is reasonable to suggest that God, as the writer of songs, can easily be extended to being the composer of the rhythms of the cosmos. A cosmos consisting of a rhythmic sea of consciousness that reverberates throughout existence. John Robinson has written

1. Songfacts, "I Write the Songs."

that "God's presence spreads through humanity like wind through quaking aspens, vibrating with the same frequency."[2]

For the many who still imagine God anthropomorphically, that is,with a corporeal body, God as rhythm may be a stretch beyond where they wish to go. Yet, this may not be all that much of a stretch. Paul described God to the Athenians as that in whom we live and breathe and have our being.[3] As early as the second century of the Christian era (CE), Irenaeus wrote about God as "all mind, all reason, all active spirit, all light."[4] In *On Providence*, Clement of Alexandria wrote "God is divine being, eternal and without beginning, incorporeal and illimitable, and the cause of what exists."[5] Origen wrote in the third century that "God, therefore, is not to be thought of as being either a body or as existing in a body, but as a simple intellectual being, admitting within himself no addition of any kind."[6] More recently, twentieth-century theologian Paul Tillich has argued that God is not a being but rather the *ground of all being found in our depth.*[7] In retrospect, God as composer of the rhythms of the cosmos, of a rhythmic sea of consciousness that reverberates throughout existence, may not be as far of a stretch as first blush may suggest.

Many moderns have a schizophrenic and, at best, muddled imagery of the Christian God. In *Life after God*, Mark Feldmeir wrote that Christianity has a God problem. He called it the elephant in the room that no one wants to talk about. He has written that "it's not a problem with God so much as it's a problem with what Christianity has made of God, how Christianity has conceived of God, and the claims that Christians have made about God."[8] The tower of beliefs discussed in chapter 2 is nowhere more prevalent than with our concept of God. We use the term to cover

2. Robinson, *I Am God*, 54.
3. Acts 17:28.
4. Irenaeus, *Against Heresies* in Schaff, *Complete Works*, loc. 26242.
5. Clement, *Book on Providence* in Schaff, *Complete Works*, loc. 17029.
6. Origen, *Fundamental Doctrines* in Schaff, *Complete Works*, loc. 38579.
7. Tillich, *Shaking of the Foundations*, 55–58.
8. Feldmeir, *Life After God*, 17.

a myriad of claims and, in polite company, we attempt to appear like we know what we are talking about. Many of our claims are contradictory and sometimes preposterous. We continue to use anthropomorphic terminology to describe a being that is in control of everything, yet chooses to remain hidden, elusive, and mysterious. In this chapter, we will consider an alternative way of thinking about God that may fit better in a world much different than the one in which God has traditionally been conceived and continues to be misunderstood.

How did this whole God thing come about? Consider this. As diverse as humanity is, we all have some things in common. We have been cursed and blessed with intellect, unlimited curiosity, and imagination, yet limited agency. At the end of our agency, we invoke our intellect and imagination and construct a higher power that we turn to for redress and insight. We commonly call this higher power *God*. The Christian God had its earliest construction among an early Hebraic tribe wandering in the Sinai. These folks were constantly under threat of being annihilated or enslaved by other tribes and death from starvation or dehydration when drought parched the land, killing them, their crops, and their livestock. They could take precautions by keeping physically strong, standing watch, taking defensive measures, and preserving water, but they could not completely mitigate these threats. Sufficient security was beyond the individual's and the tribe's agency. So, they turned to the deity YHWH for relief. YHWH was initially both a storm god and war god and fit the bill. It was to this god that they gave their allegiance. During subsequent centuries, the concept of YHWH matured as the circumstances, agency, and social structures of the Hebrew people matured.

If our understanding of God changes as human circumstances change, is the concept of God a figment of our imagination? A common saying is that there are no atheists in the foxhole. Do we imagine that a god exists out of desperation? Somewhere to turn to give us respite when in harm's way or in need of direction at a confounding turning point in life? Do we make up the concept of

God when we are at the end of our agency, just like the ancients, and have nowhere else to turn? Does God really exist?

Proof of God's existence has been attempted over the centuries. Each time, it has fallen short. Short of proof, the seventeenth-century mathematician and philosopher Blaise Pascal argued in favor of belief, that it was far better to believe in God than not to do so. His reasoning was that if one believes in God and God exists, then heaven awaits. But if you don't believe and God exists, then hell awaits. He further argued if God does not exist, there is little to gain or lose either by believing or not believing. His conclusion was that it far safer to believe in God. Pascal's argument, of course, is confounded by his own understanding of the nature of God. In the end, believing in God is a personal choice. It has been called taking a *leap of faith.* If one takes the leap, it becomes vital what one thinks about this God.

CONSTRUCTING GODS

If we take the leap and have faith in a God of reality, it makes no sense to follow a local or territorial god as the ancients did for many centuries. Nor does it make sense to have faith in an earth-centric god that lives in the heavens above the earth. It only makes sense to have faith in a God of the cosmos, of all of reality. But, while today's humans have an enhanced understanding of the cosmos and therefore have given up on storm gods and gods of war, there is still so much we do not know. So, like our early forbearers, we mentally construct our gods to find solace and peace at the limits of our agency, and to make sense of our unknowns. This is what was alluded to earlier and what Gordon Kaufman has called our *constructed god.* It is our understanding of the God of reality that we have chosen to believe in.

Throughout much of history, the cosmos was conceived as existing in three tiers.[9] One tier was the earth, the dry land on which people lived. This land was supported on pillars that kept

9. Greenwood, *Scripture and Cosmology*, 25–27.

it above the abyss of waters beneath and around it. This watery underworld was the second tier. At the ends of the earth, mountains held up the heavens where the gods lived and the sun, moon, and stars resided. There were also abundant waters in the heavens, which could be released at the god's discretion as the rain necessary for human and animal survival. This was the third tier. Within this cosmos, life was organized under monarchs, often themselves considered gods or sons of the gods. They had few restraints, and their power and prominence were omnipresent. It is within this framework that many of our current notions of God formed. We still carry remnants of these early images in our heads today. You will hear it expressed in one form or another in our worship liturgies, Scripture readings, and commentary every Sunday morning. One need not go any further than the LORD's prayer beginning with "our Father who art in heaven" to see the point being made.

While remnants remain in our worship liturgies, the three-tiered universe is now a relic of our past. Today, we have powerful telescopes and rockets that probe our solar system and beyond. Deep space probes send images to earth from a vast infinite universe that is populated with distant galaxies containing hundreds of millions of solar systems. Distances are measured in light-years measuring 5.9 trillion miles each. Our closest solar system neighbor is Alpha Centauri, which is 4.25 light-years (i.e., twenty-five trillion miles) away.[10] And the universe continues expanding. As we learn more about the cosmos, we reach further into the ultimate mystery and meaning of God.

Beyond our improved knowledge of the cosmos, we also have greater agency and control over our lives and no longer, or at least rarely, resort to superstition to make sense of things. We proactively search for solutions to our problems through the sciences, and as we gain knowledge, we less frequently resort to fate and fatalism for explanation. Yet, we still have limitations beyond our understanding and control. Here is the space for new constructs of God to develop. Yet, the old constructions die hard and linger far beyond their efficacy.

10. Astrophotography Lens, "How Far Away."

THE MUDDLED VISIONS OF THE CHRISTIAN GOD

A common image of a white-haired ancient deity with *clothing white as snow and hair like pure wool* sitting on a throne in judgment comes from the Hebrew book of Daniel.[11] It was written in the second century BCE but placed in the sixth century BCE Babylonian exile. While this early imagery persists to some extent, no clear consensus about the nature of God has surfaced to replace it. A 2006 Baylor study entitled "American Piety in the 21st Century" found four basic images of God among their subjects.[12] Nearly a third of their sample believed in an authoritarian god, a wrathful god that hates sin and sinners. Another quarter believed in a benevolent god, a caring, loving, forgiving, and healing god. Sixteen percent believed in a critical, judgmental god, one that will come to reward the holy and punish the unholy. Another quarter believed in a distant god, the clockmaker god that set the universe in motion, then stepped away and let it run on its own.

The late Marcus Borg described two understandings of God, both supported in the Bible. One is God as a supreme almighty, all-knowing being, existing beyond the universe but related to the universe as an artist is to a work of art. Another is a God that is not separate from the universe but rather a sacred presence existing all about us.[13] A common notion is that God controls all according to some divine plan that is playing out. Process theologians, building on the work of Alfred Whitehead, believe the cosmos, including God, is an interrelated wholeness that is continually growing, developing, and becoming, with an indeterminate future. In this latter scenario, God is not controlling but patiently influencing the unfolding future. Feldmeir was right, Christianity does have a God problem! Perhaps it is time to take a deep breath and consider a more basic concept for God.

11. Dan 7:9.
12. Bader et al., "American Piety."
13. Borg, *Speaking Christian*, 65.

OCCAM'S RAZOR

The fourteenth-century English theologian and philosopher William of Okham is credited with proposing that the simplest and least complex explanation for any phenomenon is preferable. A few centuries after his death, this notion became known as Occam's Razor. Consistent with this approach, theologian Paul Knitter has suggested that "everything we affirm about God, must be negated, or qualified, or cut down to size in view of what we can't say and can't know."[14] Unnecessary embellishments and justifications become suspect, and exhaustive explanations become contradictory and confounding. An open Christianity does not assume the hubris of making a leap from our current confounding and muddled understanding of God to definitively describe what is indescribable. Nor does it seek to suggest additional superlatives to further elevate our notion of God. Rather, it seeks to express a straightforward, scripturally based concept of God from a simplistic perspective that can serve as a basis for a life-giving faith.

CREATION AS A WEB OF CONSCIOUSNESS

We live and move and have our being in a vast sea of consciousness. Without consciousness, we have no concept of what is real or, for that matter, what collectively makes up reality and creation. Biologists, until recently, framed their consciousness studies around a Standard Model of Consciousness (SMC). The standard in the model was human consciousness. To determine the extent of consciousness in the cosmos, the approach was to move down the complexity of life, identifying species that had some semblance of the consciousness found in humans. An alternative and more robust approach to understanding and locating consciousness has been to start at the very bottom, from a most basic understanding of consciousness. Cellular Based Consciousness (CBC) does just that. In CBC, an entity has consciousness if it is aware of its surroundings and has the agency to appropriately respond to that

14. Knitter, *Without Buddha*, 66.

awareness.[15] The task, then, is to identify species that have both capabilities. With this approach, consciousness can be studied for its own sake, uncoupled from highly developed neural and complex brain systems of humans.

According Reber et al., even the simplest unicellular species "display behaviors that are clearly cognitive in nature including associative learning, stable memory formation, route navigation, and decision making."[16] He and his colleagues further found that they

> anticipate upcoming events and readily create functional social collectives, within which they display both cooperation and competition and, fascinatingly, a primitive form of altruism where some cells in a colony put themselves at risk to support the life functions of other cells in distress.[17]

In short, consciousness exists wherever life exists. Thus, humans exist within a conscious ecosystem of sentient beings that includes the simplest single-cell organisms as well as all flora and fauna. We need to look no further than the mutual dependency between plant and animal exchanging oxygen and carbon dioxide in support of each one's survival to deduce that we, indeed, exist in a sea of mutually dependent conscious beings.

A question that has plagued many scientists is how and when, during the unfolding of creation, did inert materials make the leap to conscious sentient beings? While many scientists remain skeptical, the ancient concept of panpsychism is receiving renewed interest. Panpsychism contends that all entities, inert or otherwise, have consciousness. That, indeed, consciousness is an endemic attribute of the universe. If this were indeed the case, there would be no need to hunt for the moment consciousness emerged, since it would have evolved from an inanimate beginning. Panpsychism was entertained in antiquity by Plato and, more recently, has been

15. Reber et al., "CBC Theory."
16. Reber et al., "CBC Theory," 8.
17. Reber et al., "CBC Theory," 8.

a matter of interest by psychologist William James and mathematician Bertrand Russel.[18] The thirteenth-century Iranian poet and Sufi mystic Rumi once wrote, "We began as a mineral. We emerged into plant life and into the animal state, and then into being human, and always we have forgotten our former states except in early spring when we slightly recall being green again."[19] In a like manner, in the same period, the German priest, theologian, and mystic Meister Eckhart argued that life is as present in a stone or a log as it is in human beings.[20] Perhaps quantum physicists or others will one day prove them correct. But it is not our task here to take sides or try to resolve this issue as it is to present a possibility. What we can propose is that the cosmos is a web of consciousness in which humans, made in the image of God, approach the status of the gods. It is within this realm of consciousness that an open Christianity can begin to conceive of a construct for God that can serve us today.

AN OPEN CHRISTIAN FOUNDATION FOR GOD

We have already discussed the confusion surrounding the Christian God. This is in part due to conflicting biblical depictions of God. Biblical descriptions growing out of the earliest form of a rain and war god include Joshua's depiction of a warrior god that empowered his armies to victories and even the slaughter of every living thing in the city-states he allegedly conquered. I say "allegedly" because Judges gives a less gory account of the establishment of the Hebrew kingdom, as does contemporary archaeological evidence.[21] The prophets and parts of the Pentateuch depict a god of love and justice that does not condemn the Hebrews when they stray but allowed them to experience the consequences of their actions, and, with love, accepted them back into his caring

18. Skrbina, *Panpsychism in the West.*
19. Rumi, *Essential Rumi*, 113.
20. Eckhart, *Complete Mystical Works*, 173, 208, 248, 300, 352, 404–5.
21. Dever, *What Did the Biblical Writers*, 122.

guidance. Jesus's first-century reforms picked up on the wisdom of the prophets and extended it to form the basis of Christianity and a God of love.

Perhaps today's confusion surrounding God stems from an insistence by some Christians on an infallible and literal interpretation of Scripture. In such a mindset, all descriptions of God in Scripture have equal weight, no matter how incompatible they may be. An open Christianity understands Scripture as a journey through which the concept of God evolves and matures, culminating in Jesus's loving parental imagery. It is with this in mind that the following open Christian understanding of God is offered.

God is the ubiquitous, perfectly loving consciousness mentoring the cosmos.

This ubiquitous, perfectly loving consciousness is everywhere, all the time, the very reality in which we live and breathe and have our being. No long beard, woolly hair, or corporeal body but an ever-present spiritual grounding that is undergirding existence.

GOD OF LOVE

In 1 Corinthians, Paul wrote a profound and beautiful description of love. It is often recited in wedding ceremonies and as tributes to a deceased person at their funeral or memorial service. I recited Paul's poem of love at my parents' and wife's parents' memorial services. Paul's description of love is the Christian standard for the meaning of love. He wrote the following.

> Love is patient; love is kind; love is not envious or boastful or arrogant or rude. It does not insist on its own way; it is not irritable; it keeps no record of wrongs; it does not rejoice in wrongdoing but rejoices in the truth. It bears all things, believes all things, hopes all things, endures all things. Love never ends.[22]

How would Paul's love apply to God? Could there be two standards for love? One for God and one for God's people? I think

22. 1 Cor 4–8.

that would only add further confusion to an understanding of God than we have today. If Paul's inspired poem of love is accurate, as I believe it is, then God, as perfect loving consciousness, must also follow that path hewn by Paul. What does this imply?

We can certainly rule out God being an authoritarian, wrathful god that hates sin and sinners. That would be inconsistent with Paul's attributes of love. We can also rule out a distant god, a clockmaker god setting the universe in motion then stepping away. That would be a cold, unfeeling, disinterested, and aloof deity inconsistent with perfect love. Nor would it be a critical and judgmental god, holding grudges and desiring to punish wrongdoing. Paul's love has no room for keeping a record of wrongs and rejoicing in wrongdoing. It would not be an almighty, all-knowing god, existing beyond the universe but dabbling with the universe as though creating a work of art. That would be abandonment, not love.

It could not be a god that can only accept the crucifixion of his beloved son as a means of reconciling with sinful humans. Nor could an open Christian god, following Paul's vision of love, send sinners to hell for eternity or have a judgment day. Nor could a god imbued with Paul's love control all events in human history or follow a rigid, immutable, nonsensical plan that is an explanation of why bad things happen to good people, from the death of a child to the path of a devastating killer storm or a fatal automobile accident. In an open Christian theology, God's plan is simply evolving a future through love, with inspiration in place of control, patience in place of anger, and forgiveness in place of retribution. There is no judgment day, no end times, no rapture. There is the endless evolution of humans becoming more loving and God-like.

The perfectly loving God in an open Christianity, following Paul's 1 Cor description, would be like the quarter of the Baylor study's subjects understanding of God as a benevolent, caring, and loving deity promoting forgiveness and healing. And not unlike Borg's panentheistic understanding of God, not separate from the universe but, rather, as a sacred presence existing all about us. It is consistent with Paul's description to the Athenians and the process theologians' belief of a God not controlling but, rather, patiently influencing the unfolding future. This is the God of an open Christianity.

AN INVITATION TO TRANSCENDENCE

History is a story of God consciously evolving, experimenting, and patiently influencing reality, all wrapped in a burrito or blanket of love. This consciousness invites us into the fullness of being, into an abundant life, and into transcendence. God invites us as well as all existence to transcend what is and create new things and become new beings, sometimes seemingly out of nothing, out of what appears as chaos, or other times, through evolving what already exists into something even better. This invitation to transcendence is what *being* is about and what God is the grounding of. *Being* means participating in the evolution of creation. Our agency, or choice, is to accept or reject God's invitation into abundant being and conscious awareness. It is sensing the rhythm of the web of consciousness and dancing with the intrinsic music of creation. It is working with God, residing in our depth, as co-creators in the quest for perfection in all things, including what it means to be fully human. But what does this look like? How do we distinguish between what seems like God's rhythmic consciousness but may only be our own ego-driven motivation? It would surely be helpful to have a concrete example of one who has lived such a life, and from whom we can learn the way. For Christians, that example is the life and teaching of the first-century Jesus of Nazareth. But like the confounding images that have plagued our understanding of God, the imagery we have of Jesus has also been confounded. In chapter 4, we will address some of these confounding factors and propose an understanding of Jesus that can form a basis for an open Christianity today.

THOUGHT EXERCISES

1. How have you envisioned God in your lifetime? Has this changed over the years?
2. Does the distinction between the real God and a constructed God make sense to you?
3. Has it ever occurred to you, as Feldmeir says, that Christianity has a God problem?
4. What do you think of God not as a being but the ground of being?
5. What does God as ubiquitous loving consciousness mean to you?

4

Jesus

When he entered Jerusalem, the whole city was in turmoil, asking, Who is this?

MATTHEW 21:10

OPEN CHRISTIANITY, DECONSTRUCTED OF extraordinary claims and taking a candid approach to claims about Jesus, places us in the same position of those first-century Jerusalemites at Passover, asking, "Who is this man?" What should we in the twenty-first century think of this Jesus? What claims, if any, should we believe about him? Should we believe he is the very son of God, the second person of the Holy Trinity? Did he bring back people from the dead? Did he, himself, come back from the dead? Did he heal the sick, give sight to the blind, feed the multitude with a meager allotment of fishes and loaves, calm the seas, and walk on water? Did he free a demonic of evil spirits and release them into a herd of pigs at Gerasenes? Did he ascend to heaven forty days after his crucifixion, as reported in the book of Acts? Was he the incarnation of God, a son with whom God was well pleased? If so, why was this person crucified as a criminal, traitor, and insurrectionist?

Today, Jesus is venerated by many as the savior of humankind, as the very son of God. Yet, all that we know about him has been written by his fans, followers, and apologists. It was written in the genre of the first century, in which it was commonplace to attribute miraculous events to notable people and cast them as gods or children of gods. We simply do not have an objective, unbiased account of who this man was. Given all of this, how should we understand claims made about this Jesus today that, for many, seem preposterous? Should these claims be taken literally? Or should we look more deeply into the Gospel authors' intentions of promoting Jesus during a very difficult time for the Jewish people and Judaism itself?

My Christian journey and introduction to Jesus began with infant baptism at St. Mark's Lutheran Church in Butler, Pennsylvania, on February 7, 1943. It is the church where my great-grandparents, both German immigrants, were married. It is also where their oldest child, my grandmother, was baptized and later married my grandfather, and where my father and brother were also baptized. I was nine weeks old at the time. Just shy of a year later, my father was drafted by the army and sent to fight on the front lines in WWII's Northern Italian campaign. On October 30, 1944, he was wounded in action and spent the next several months recuperating in a military hospital in Italy. Dad recovered from his wounds and was discharged from the army on October 21, 1945. The experience of war, like it had for so many, softened Dad's interest in the church for many years, until it rekindled in his retirement years. As a result, my understanding of Jesus came in bits and spurts over the subsequent decades and mostly from a literalist perspective. For me, Jesus was set on such a high pedestal that rather than be inspired and try to emulate him, I felt guilt and inadequacy. Yet, strangely, perhaps drawn from my father's influence, I also had a healthy measure of skepticism. It was in my twenties that I began to act on that skepticism, deconstruct my literal beliefs, and then in my early thirties, I began serious study of Christian writers and theologians. It was during this time that I began looking into the mythology surrounding Jesus more deeply than the earlier literal approach could provide. I have been on that journey ever since, worshiping, studying, reading, and experiencing matters of faith. I reached the point of deeply admiring Jesus and doing my best to model myself after him. To reach that point, I believe it is helpful to understand why and how these extraordinary claims about Jesus were fashioned. With such an understanding, I believe one can reach a deeper understanding than is possible through literal reading.

There are claims we can accept about Jesus that I believe are indisputable. The first is that Jesus had a charismatic personality and an ability to speak so compellingly that people were easily drawn to him. Second, his persona, teachings, and integrity had a profound impact upon his followers that even his death could not destroy. Third, he sought to reform early first-century Judaism. This latter point is clear from Matthew's chapter 5, with several passages beginning with the words, "It has been said, but I say . . ." Further, the distinction between reform and replacement becomes clear in Matthew when Jesus said, "Do not think I have come to abolish the Law or the Prophets; I have come not to abolish them but to fulfill them."[1] And to further lay out the essence of fulfilling the Law and prophets, Jesus drew from Deuteronomy and Leviticus, indicating that fulfillment comes by loving God and neighbor with all your heart, mind, and soul. Jesus said that "on these two commandments hang all the Law and the Prophets."[2] Unfortunately, in the first century of the Christian era, these qualities of charismatic teaching and religious reform set Jesus up for an untimely and excruciating crucifixion.

The two overwhelming sources of power in first-century Israel were the Roman overlords and the temple cult. Jesus's charisma and outspokenness threatened both. Any charismatic that could attract a crowd would raise the suspicion of the Roman authorities as a potential threat. Reforming society is a dangerous undertaking, as evidenced by the early violent deaths of Dietrich Bonhoeffer, Mahatma Gandhi, John F. Kennedy, Robert Kennedy, Martin Luther King Jr., and Malcolm X. An attempt to reform a powerful religious cult, such as Jerusalem's temple power structure, was even more likely to end in violence. In this crucible of first-century

1. Matt 5:17.
2. Matt 22:40.

Israel, it was inevitable that Jesus would meet an untimely death through the horror of crucifixion.

But, after his death, how and why did the claims about this Jesus reach such a level that, in today's post supernaturalism mentality, would seem outrageous? What is the justification for this and how did it come about? This is what we are going to consider next. We will look at three considerations: (1) the stigma of crucifixion; (2) the first-century literary genre used for expressing the inexpressible; and (3) an effort by Jesus's followers to replace the temple cult with the Jesus cult.

THE CRUCIFIXION STIGMA—JUSTIFICATION FOR HYPERBOLE

At the beginning of the first century of the Christian era (CE), Israel was an agricultural society, in which all but a very small percentage of people lived at the subsistence level in extended family compounds. Illness or death of a key member of the community, or one of many other potential misfortunes, placed the whole extended community in jeopardy. One of those other misfortunes could come from bandits and looters roaming the countryside, threatening the survival of the extended family communes. These groups were also not above making a statement against Rome by attacking vulnerable Roman officials. In these times, any attack on a Roman official would be considered an attack on Rome itself. In retribution, and to set an example, the iron fist of Rome would come down on the broader peasant population. Crucifixion was Rome's preferred deterrent for such attacks. And because of the multiple threats that the bandits posed, crucifixion had broad public support.[3]

Crucifixion was a brutal form of capital punishment.[4] Dying victims hung on a crudely made cross, slowly and shamefully suffocating from the pull of gravity upon their weakened and often

3. Hengel, *Crucifixion*, loc. 1330–36.

4. For more on crucifixion, see Hengel, *Crucifixion*.

naked bodies. After death, their bodies hung on the crosses for several more days, setting an example for others, while birds of prey and wild animals fed on their corpses. Finally, what was left of them would be cut down and thrown into a garbage pit. All that having been said, crucifixion had a fair amount of support among the populace. It was a deterrent to marauding bandits that could steal a community's livelihood or for insurrectionists that could indiscriminately bring the Roman boot down on a small community or the entire population. It is within this context that this man Jesus, who had caught the hearts and souls of many followers, ended his life.

Bart Ehrman posed the obvious question: "Why would anyone pay attention to this man?" Ehrman continued, "For most first-century Jews, to call Jesus the Messiah was ludicrous at best, blasphemous at worst. Nothing could be crazier, no one could be less messianic, than a crucified criminal."[5] Clearly, to overcome the crucifixion stigma, Jesus's biographers, on whom he had such a compelling impact, used hyperbolic language expressed in supernatural language to counter that impact. But would Jesus have used the supernatural to deliver his message? Evidence suggests otherwise.

AN EXPERIENCE BEYOND WORDS

Paul's letters are the earliest documents we have regarding the impact Jesus had on his followers. He was born Saul in Tarsus around the beginning of the first century. He became a Pharisee and an avid persecutor of early Christians. On such a mission, he was struck with a powerful vision on the road to Damascus around 36 CE. For the remainder of his life, he became known as Paul and a devoted missionary, establishing Christian communities around the Mediterranean. There are seven uncontested letters Paul wrote to these communities that have survived and are part of the Christian New Testament. The earliest is believed to have been written

5. Ehrman, *Jesus Interrupted*, 87.

about 50 CE. His life ended in execution about 66 CE by Nero during the latter's persecution of Christians.[6]

Paul's letters provided much of the grist for Christian theology. Interestingly, he had little to say about the biographical Jesus, and while he made strong claims about the meaning of Jesus, he never mentioned any of the miracles found in the Gospels. It is the Gospels that provide the biographical details of the life and teachings of Jesus. Three of the Gospels (Mark, Matthew, Luke) are referred to as the Synoptic Gospels. They were written within a period of approximately fifteen to twenty-five years, beginning some forty years after the crucifixion.[7] Synoptic comes from the word "synopsis," meaning an overview or general perspective on a particular topic, in this case, the life and teaching of Jesus. The final Gospel, John, written later than the Synoptics, differs in that, with additional time, John put the life of Jesus in a more philosophical and theological framework. While Mark doesn't mention the birth of Jesus, and both Matthew and Luke added a virginal birth narrative, John gives Jesus an eternal presence, as the *Word* or *Logos*, and as the very essence and Spirit of God. Further, while Mark, Matthew, and Luke all provide a profile of Jesus's life and teaching, they all differ in some respects. It is not our task here to flesh out those differences but rather to point out that differences occurred because different people wrote about their personal understanding of Jesus within the context of his impact upon them and others. As such, the Gospels should be read independently and should not be mixed or thrown together to form a Christian stew, as though they are each addressing identical experiences.

Further, the experiences being relayed in the Gospels are an attempt to express what is inexpressible. Words just don't exist, or at least don't come easily, to express what one feels deeply within their hearts. It was true for the ancient Gospel writers as it is true for us today. There are experiences that just defy written description. Miracles, common to the genre of the day, were a vehicle Gospel writers used to stretch human language to describe

6. Borg and Crossan, *First Paul*, 14.

7. Sheehan, *First Coming*, 21.

what they had experienced in Jesus.[8] The Gospels are not the only example of this. Apollonius of Tyana was a first-century venerated Greek philosopher and religious leader whose life also took on a mythical character.[9] He was said to have been born of a virgin, healed the sick, brought people back from the dead, and after his death, ascended to heaven. Emperor Augustus himself was given the titles LORD, savior of the world, and son of God to honor his victory over Mark Antony's forces and usher in the Pax Romana. The point is that what may seem like extraordinary claims today were not uncommon in the first century, and so, to take them literally would be misleading.

Perhaps, it would be better to look at the supernatural claims from a bit more distance. Jesus was a game changer. The Gospels are quite clear that Jesus's reforms were contrary to many of Judaism's beliefs and practices in his day. For example, Jesus did not teach that illness and impoverishment were God's punishment for the unworthy or that wealth and good health were God's rewards for the holy. His healing the sick, whether actual or metaphorical, eating with sinners of his day, and touching the untouchables were not just actions but also religious and political statements. He did not believe in an ostentatious display of religiosity, such as loud public praying on street corners. Instead, he taught about service and humility. His concerns were where the rubber hits the road, i.e., on outcomes and actions, such as feeding the hungry, clothing the naked, slaking thirst, and so forth. It was by their fruits one was to be known. The impoverished, physically and mentally ill, and victims of misfortune were not to be condemned for getting what they deserved (i.e., God's punishment for sinfulness). Rather, Jesus's behavior and teaching was a foundation for today's building of social safety nets, educational institutions, hospitals, and scientific laboratories, all to address problems and difficulties faced by the human family. And, at best, this is to be done not for personal gain but through love that transcends the satisfaction of,

8. Spong, *Jesus for the Non-Religious*, 95.

9. Guthrie, *Gospel of Apollonius of Tyana*; Philostratus, *Life of Apollonius of Tyana.*

and perhaps even at the expense of, one's own physiological and psychological needs.

At the time of the writing of the Gospel of Mark, the first Jewish-Roman war was in full swing. Some believe Mark was written after the fall of Jerusalem in 70 CE.[10] If so, the nation's treasure and people had fallen to the Romans. Jerusalem's wealth and much of its surviving population were removed to Rome, which provided financial and human resources for the future building of the Colosseum. Even if Mark was written prior to Jerusalem's fall, the handwriting was on the wall, and the inevitable crumble of traditional Judaism practice easily foreseen. Thus, with the destruction of the temple, either a *fait accompli* or imminent, an opening occurred regarding what would replace the temple power structure within Judaism. One possibility is that it could restructure itself into the rabbinical form it has today. Another possibility is that the cult of Jesus could provide the path to God that had previously been fulfilled by the temple cult. It was within this context that the followers of Jesus sought to replace the destroyed temple cult with Jesus as a new pathway to God. But to be successful, the narrative for making Jesus the *new path* would have to be couched in the context of Jewish history and tradition. Jesus would need to be introduced and explained within a traditional Jewish religious foundation.

Hence, Matthew began his Gospel with a genealogy tying Jesus through several generations back to Abraham, the founder of the faith. Luke 3 goes further, tying Jesus's heritage back to Adam. While both genealogies have their questionable veracity and their own purposes, they nonetheless attempt to place Jesus as the progeny of Judaism's heritage. The birth of Jesus in Bethlehem, the city of David, reported in both Matthew and Luke, is a clear reference to Mic 5:2, i.e., the Messiah coming from Bethlehem. Matthew's account of Herod ordering the killing of all children under the age of two would certainly, for Jews, harken back to Egypt's Pharaoh ordering midwives in his country to kill all male children born to Jewish women. Jews would relate Jesus's walking on water and

10. Sheehan, *First Coming*, 21.

calming the seas with Moses parting the Red Sea. Jesus turning water into wine would be compared to Moses turning the bitter water sweet, and Jesus feeding the multitudes with a few loaves and fishes would recount Moses's manna from heaven or Elijah multiplying the meal and oil of the widow at Zarephath. Jesus raising Lazarus from the dead would recall Elijah raising the widow's son from death. Another parallel of note is Moses's validation on the mountain receiving the Ten Commandments and Jesus's transfiguration on the mountain. Accompanied by Peter, James, and John, Jesus "was transfigured before them, and his face shone like the sun, and his clothes became bright as light." Moses and Elijah appeared and "suddenly a bright cloud overshadowed them, and a voice from the cloud said, 'This is my Son, the Beloved; with him I am well pleased; listen to him!'"[11] Those are some incredibly compelling references for becoming the new face of Judaism. However, it wasn't enough, and the rabbinical framework is what ultimately sustained the Jews after the destruction of the temple cult.

THE JESUS CULT AND THE GENTILES

While Jesus did not become the new pathway to God for most Jews, his followers did find rich ground among the gentiles. Many gentiles in the Diaspora respected the Jew's monotheism, morality, and family values. In many cases, they were even financial benefactors of the synagogues. These gentiles were known as the *Godfearers* and were fertile ground for the early Christian missionaries. That is where it prospered and grew. Unfortunately, being unfamiliar with the Jewish heritage and scriptural meaning, much of the Gospel writings were understood literally rather within the Judeo scriptural context.[12] In subsequent decades, centuries, and millennia came creeds, dogma, and doctrine making claims about Jesus being the Son of God, the second person of the Holy Trinity, and even of the very same substance as God. Various atonement

11. Matt 17:2–5; also in Mark 9:2–7.

12. Spong, *Jesus for the Non-Religious*,149.

theories have surfaced over the centuries to explain how a powerful god could permit his only beloved son be crucified. Today, some Christian bodies contend that declaring Jesus as one's personal LORD and Savior punches their ticket to eternity in heaven. In other cases, being Christian today has become a matter of accepting creedal beliefs and faith statements about who Jesus is rather than internalizing his essence of loving self-transcendence.

An open Christianity eschews propagating first-century genre claims about Jesus as actual historical events but rather focus on the depth of Jesus's message, both taught and lived. If we just take a deep breath, do we not know that Jesus was an exceptional human being who lived a courageous and authentic life all the way to his death? Is it all that difficult to accept that he had an exceptional vision of God that he passed on to us? Is it necessary to resort to supernaturalism or magic to comprehend the nature and legitimacy of Jesus and his message? Is there need to, like Thomas, place our fingers into the wounds of Jesus's body to internalize and believe in his message? As Scripture implies in John 20, blessed are those who *get it, know it, and internalize it* without hardcore evidence, simply because we know the alternative to love and have lived it for centuries. The real essence of Jesus lies not in supernatural beliefs about who he was or did but in internalizing and expressing his essence in our lives.

WHO WAS THIS MAN JESUS?

With all of this said, can we discern from Scripture, perhaps with help from contemporary leadership models and common sense, a more realistic and less supernatural picture of this man called Jesus? Let's begin by asking what Jesus believed about himself, or perhaps the better question, who did Jesus decide to become? Therefore, it is appropriate to reopen the question, "Who was this man Jesus?" We will begin with what preceded his ministry, namely, his baptism by John the Baptist in the Jordan and his time in the wilderness.

Prophets and, for that matter, all successful leaders begin with a vision, a mystical awareness of a beneficial *future state of affairs* and a role one might have in bringing it about. The future state may be pertaining to one's own self, as in one's career hopes or desires for future material well-being. But in a grander arena, that future state of affairs will pertain to the well-being of others, perhaps even the whole of humankind. It is what drives some to become teachers, researchers, and political or religious leaders. A pastor may have a future state of affairs in mind for her congregation or community. But where does this mystical awareness or vision come from? Do visions come from our randomly wandering semiconscious dreams, our unstructured musings, from random firings of brain synapses and neurotransmitters? Do they come from God? Is it, as Richard Rohr has written, "a jumping on board, a divine flow that we step into, a holy plank that we walk into an infinite but good unknown"?[13]

Visions, in the true sense, are new creations. They are not simply electrical pulses pulled out of memory cells and merely reorganized into some alternate form. They often appear in a flash, at least in part, but mature over a longer period. They have their own wholeness, more than the sum of their parts, and are often difficult to express. Their full expression requires more than words; actions are also needed for a vision to be fully expressed, evident, and understood. Visions are indeed a mystery that we experience within the sea of consciousness. I am pretty sure that Jesus had a vision, and he was convinced it came from God's ubiquitous consciousness. It pertained to Jesus's vision of God's essence as the *epitome of human perfection.* I believe it was this vision that formed the basis for Jesus's teaching and life example. It is what early Christian doctrines were expressing when they said Jesus was the "son of God."

I believe that God's essence is the perfection and divinity into which humans can evolve, and Jesus sought to be the example of it, illustrating in word and deed what it is. In other words, God's divinity would be found in the fully evolved human, and Jesus had the vision of what that was like. This is the vision that Jesus became.

13. Rohr, *Tears*, 79.

We don't know when Jesus received his vision. It may have come gradually over time in his pre-missionary years, as he matured into manhood, or it may have come in a flash. What we do know is that his vision was validated as John baptized him in the Jordan. Mark, Matthew, and Luke all report this in their Gospels. Matthew reported that when he came out of the water, "suddenly the heavens were opened to him, and he saw God's Spirit descending like a dove and alighting on him. And a voice from the heavens said, 'This is my Son, the Beloved, with whom I am well pleased.'"[14]

Visions are feckless unless they are acted upon. What would be Jesus's next step after receiving this vision and having it validated? How did he expect to bring it to fruition? What was his approach to be? What path would Jesus take to embody his vision and pursue his mission? How would he implement it? What was his strategy? To answer that, we shall return to the Gospel accounts of his time in the wilderness. Reading between the lines, it was here that Jesus worked out his approach to ministry, his teaching, and life example. And it wasn't through miracles and supernaturalism.

THE WILDERNESS AND SERVANT LEADERSHIP

How would Jesus, with his vision of what it means to be fully human and desire to bring abundant life to his followers, proceed? What would it mean? Would it mean modeling the messianic hopes of his people? Would it require throwing off the yoke of Rome's hegemony? Would it mean calling on God for supernatural miracles to address and satisfy the needs of his people? Would he use his charisma to raise a mighty army to bring together all the people of the world under a Jewish regime? All important considerations and legitimate options. In solitude today, we turn to wilderness experiences when we must consider our alternatives and set a direction. Scripture reports that Jesus at once went into the wilderness to ponder his options and determine his style of ministry.

14. Matt 3:16–17.

All four Gospels report on his wilderness experience. Mark characteristically has the most cryptic account, stating only that "the Spirit immediately drove him out into the wilderness. He was in the wilderness forty days, tested by Satan, and he was with the wild beasts, and the angels waited on him."[15] Matthew is a bit more explicit and Luke's account mirrors it except for exchanging the sequencing of the second and third temptations. Both accounts describe three of the considerations that Jesus rejected: turning stones into bread to assuage his hunger, throwing himself off the temple to supernaturally test God's support, and becoming the political ruler of kingdoms of the world. It is as though Jesus's thinking regarding these strategies was that the message and image of full humanity supersede temporarily satisfying the desires and immediate needs of his people, the momentary thrill of performing supernatural acts, or the futility finding peace and abundant life in a setting of political hegemony. It was the vision of full humanity that had to become his very essence, that vision he had of God's fully human dimension.[16]

Here are several takeaways coming from the accounts of Jesus's wilderness experience. First, Jesus would not prioritize satisfying his own personal needs for sustenance, shelter, or other creaturely comforts. He would not, as it were, change the stone into bread to satisfy his hunger. Rather, Jesus chose the role of servant, a role he often elevated in sayings such as "The greatest among you will be your servant. All who exalt themselves will be humbled, and all who humble themselves will be exalted."[17] Second, Jesus would not rely on supernatural spectacles to give credence to his message. He would not put the LORD his God to the test. Third, he would not follow a path of first-century messianic expectations. He chose to not serve the false idols of political power and military force but only serve God.

15. Mark 1:12–13.

16. Karl Barth argued for the humanity of God in his lecture delivered at the Swiss Reformed Ministers' Association in Aarau, Switzerland, September 25, 1956.

17. Matt 23:11–12; also Mark 10:45, Matt 20:28, and Luke 22:26–27.

SERVANT LEADERSHIP

Jesus exemplified what is now called a *servant leadership* model. Robert Greenleaf introduced the term in his 1970 essay "The Servant as Leader." According to the Center for Servant Leadership,

> A servant-leader focuses primarily on the growth and well-being of people and the communities to which they belong. While traditional leadership generally involves the accumulation and exercise of power by one at the "top of the pyramid," servant leadership is different. The servant-leader shares power, puts the needs of others first and helps people develop and perform as highly as possible.[18]

Servant leaders empower their followers to find new sources of power and skill within themselves. It is within this often-inexpressible experience that the Gospel authors resorted to the first-century miracle genre to explain Jesus. We don't know if Jesus was the first to model servant leadership, but from what is known about leadership examples in the ancient world, he may well have been. We do know that it seems to have fallen out of use after Jesus's modeling of it. Servant leadership, at its very best, prioritizes the selfless pursuit of mission. Releasing the grip of the ego releases a power of certainty and of determination that can stand the testing for what lies ahead.

THE ENIGMA OF THE SON OF MAN

Much has been made of Jesus's divinity over the centuries. It has been said he is the son of God, of the same substance as God, and the second person in the Trinity. However, there are almost no claims of Jesus calling himself divine or messiah. Where that has occurred, scholars now believe that the words were not his but rather put in his mouth by admirers.[19] Jesus did refer to himself

18. Robert K. Greenleaf Center for Servant Leadership, "What Is Servant Leadership?," para. 4.

19. Wink, *Human Being*, 19.

frequently in the Gospels as the *son of man.* In fact, he refers to himself as this over a total of eighty times in the four Gospels. Further, Jesus is the only one in Scripture that refers to himself as such. But what does this mean?

Traditionally, it has been believed to refer to the *son of man* reference in chapter 7 of Daniel. Daniel has two major themes. One is Daniel's experience as a high-level officer in the Babylonian government. The story of Daniel in the lion's den is found here. The other is an apocalyptic vision of how God will send "one like a son of man," given "dominion and glory and kingship, that all peoples, nations, and languages should serve him."[20]

This theme certainly matches with themes in the New Testament book of Revelation. It has also been used to bolster assertions for Jesus's divinity. But does it really line up with the Gospels, where Jesus modeled servant leadership and empowering others in love? It doesn't seem like a good fit, nor is it a good fit with Jesus eschewing a messianic role in the wilderness account. Perhaps we should look elsewhere for the meaning of "son of man."

Walter Wink provides a compelling argument for another explanation for the son of man attribution.[21] It is found in the book of Ezekiel. While Daniel was cast in the time of the Babylonian exile, it was written four hundred years later, after the exile. Ezekiel, on the other hand, lived during the early time of the Babylonian exile. His task was to keep a remanent Judaism alive. While his prophesy ranted about the sins of his people, after time, he received in part this vision from God:

> A new heart I will give you, and a new spirit I will put within you, and I will remove from your body the heart of stone and give you a heart of flesh.[22]

This seems very much in accord with the career of Jesus in the Gospels. In Ezekiel's visions, God refers to him as the "son of man." God addresses Ezekiel as a son of man not once or twice but

20. Dan 7:14.

21. Wink, *Human Being*, 19–39.

22. Ezek 36:26.

over ninety times. It is to emphasize that Ezekiel is a mortal chosen to receive visions from God. It would seem consistent to think that Jesus referred to himself as the "son of man," a mortal, as within the context of Ezekiel, and not the context of Daniel.

While attempts have been made in biblical passages, post-biblical creeds, dogmas, and doctrines to establish Jesus as divine, he did not speak of himself in elevated terms. In those cases where he does seem to elevate himself, one must wonder, given the evidence considered so far, if they are really words from his own mouth or whether they are part of the hyperbola that later engulfed his legacy, as we have earlier suggested.

Jesus had a vision of God that exemplified fully developed humanity. And that is what Jesus made manifest through his teaching and life example. He saw himself not as divine but, rather, as a son of man with a vision from God of what it means to be fully and completely human. In Mark, Jesus says, "Why do you call me good? No one is good but God alone."[23] Thus, he was not considering himself divine but rather striving to exemplify what it means to live the fully human life according to his vision of God's complete humanness.

PASSING THE FINAL TEST

Luke ends his account of the wilderness experience with the words "When the devil had finished every test, he departed from him until an opportune time."[24] And that opportune time was in the garden, the Garden of Gethsemane, where Jesus's denial of self and his servanthood was ultimately tested. On his cross, Jesus made the final leap in self-transcendence, himself becoming fully human. John ends Jesus's life with these words, "'It is finished.' Then he bowed his head and gave up his spirit."[25]

23. Mark 10:18.
24. Luke 4:13.
25. John 19:30.

A few years ago, my wife and I visited Israel and walked through the Garden of Gethsemane. It was here, of course, that Satan's final challenge was issued and that Jesus's integrity was deeply and existentially tested. Ancient olive trees stand in the garden, and one particularly gnarled and ancient one, we were told, was old enough to have been there that evening Jesus had his last opportunity to bail out on his mission. For us, the present day was touching the past as we walked through the garden. In this very garden, under the intense pressure of impending crucifixion, would he crumble and flee back to Galilee into retirement and a quieter life? Or would he maintain his integrity and face his impending future? We know the outcome. In deep duress, speaking to his God, he said out loud, "My Father, if it is possible, let this cup pass from me, yet not what I want but what you want."[26] We know the rest of the story. He not only taught and lived his understanding of God's hope and desire, but he also kept the faith until his ending. Is it any wonder the story ends with a resurrection? The eternal truth expressed by Jesus cannot be snuffed out, as John wrote in his Gospel, or lay dormant in some tomb. John wrote, "In him was life, and the life was the light of all people. The light shines in the darkness, and the darkness did not overtake it."[27] The truth of Jesus could not be snuffed out by death on a cross. The body of Jesus was crucified, but the truth and essence of Jesus is resurrected every time we choose to follow his path.

ATONEMENT[28]

The crucifixion not only caused the early Christian apologists to do a heap of explaining, often resorting to feats of supernaturalism, but for those who became followers, the question to resolve was why God would have let such a thing happen. To answer this

26. Matt 26:39.

27. John 1:4–5.

28. For a more detailed discussion of atonement, see Gould, *Being Christian*, 44–55.

question, it is informative to understand the transactional relationship humankind has and continues to have with their God.

It may have been common practice, but an early example is in the eighth chapter of Genesis. Noah, fresh off the boat, sent delightful aromas heavenward from a burnt offering to appease an angry God, the God that had just tried to kill every living thing on earth other than Noah's small contingent. And it worked. Afterwards, God vowed that he would never repeat that act. Appeasing God with sacrifices of burnt offerings, accompanied by the burning of incense and appointed festivals, became big business in ancient Israel as well as other ancient societies. But how does the crucifixion fit into all of this?

Before this is addressed, it is helpful to understand Augustine's role. In the fourth century, Saint Augustine, drawing on the *original sin* of Adam and Eve eating from the forbidden tree of knowledge, wrote extensively about the depraved nature of mankind. He argued that this original sin tainted all of humanity, that humans were indeed born in sin.[29] If we think of an all-powerful, angry God, how could crucifying his only son do anything but make God angrier?

The theory of substitutional sacrifice, still front and center in Christian doctrine today, came to us from the middle ages. It states that humankind had nothing of sufficient value to sacrifice to God that could atone for their history of depravity and sinfulness. The only thing of sufficient value to atone for these sins was God's only son. Jesus, therefore, became the sacrificial substitute that could reconcile God with humanity.

An open Christianity thinks of the crucifixion differently. Crucifixion is the outcome of radical, transcendent love confronting societal injustice. Atonement is not attained with transactional sacrifices. Chapter 1 of Isaiah is clear about this.

> I have had enough of burnt offerings of rams and the fat of fed beasts; I do not delight in the blood of bulls or of lambs or of goats. . . . Bringing offerings is futile; incense

29. Augustine, *St. Augustine of Hippo*, bk. 14.

> is an abomination to me . . . and your appointed festivals my soul hates.[30]

Micah is equally clear about this.

> With what shall I come before the LORD and bow myself before God on high? Shall I come before him with burnt offerings, with calves a year old? Will the LORD be pleased with thousands of rams, with ten thousands of rivers of oil? Shall I give my firstborn for my transgression, the fruit of my body for the sin of my soul?[31]

Both Isaiah's and Micah's atonement messages are clear.

> Wash yourselves; make yourselves clean; remove your evil deeds from before my eyes; cease to do evil; learn to do good; seek justice; rescue the oppressed; defend the orphan; plead for the widow.[32] What does the LORD require of you but to do justice and to love kindness and to walk humbly with your God?[33]

In an open Christianity, atonement is not transactional. It cannot be bought with sacrifices, nor can we accept Jesus's ugly death as a substitute bartered for forgiveness of our own imperfections. An open Christianity will not believe we are washed "white as snow with the blood of Jesus," as the hymn suggests.[34] What an open Christian does believe is that confronting injustice carries risks. The transcendent person, i.e., one willing to put seeking truth and pursuing justice above self-satisfaction, is walking with God in atonement. The walk is not complicated or convoluted; it simply consists of humbly seeking justice and acting kindly. The walk is not transactional; it is transcendental, the giving one's very self in the archetype of Jesus. It is not a "Jesus paid it all" doctrine; it is "Jesus cut the path" mindset. In an open Christianity, the cross symbolizes this and reminds us of our faith commitment.

30. Isa 1:11–14.
31. Mic 6:6–7.
32. Isa 1:16–17.
33. Mic 6:8.
34. Mowery, "Whiter Than Snow."

CORNERSTONE THE BUILDERS REJECTED

King David, in Ps 118, somewhat feeling his oats, thanked God for having faith in him and making him the cornerstone that many of his contemporaries and superiors had rejected. Jesus, in each of the Synoptic Gospels refers, to himself as the cornerstone that the builders (i.e., religious leaders) rejected. A cornerstone is the stone initially laid that determines the true integrity of a structure. Jesus's reforms, contained in his teachings and life example, were meant to be the cornerstone of a renewed Judaism. Instead, they became the foundation for Christianity. Additional supernatural claims, extraordinary creeds, doctrines, and dogmas, while still venerated and meaningful for many, are unnecessary for the open Christian. The following statement is the only assertion about Jesus in an open Christianity.

Jesus's teaching and life example demonstrate God's full and perfect humanity, providing a visionary path for us individually and collectively to evolve into becoming fully human.

Over half a century ago, Rufus Jones put it this way: "We have at last seen in him what man was meant to be . . . the divine possibilities of the human nature we bear."[35]

Open Christians trust that Jesus was the way, the truth, and the life and that following his example and teaching will lead to a life atoned with God. With Jesus as Christianity's cornerstone, in the next chapter, we will turn to a discussion of being human, swimming in God's perfectly loving sea of consciousness in this twenty-first century.

THOUGHT EXERCISES

1. Have you thought about how crucifixion might have been thought of in Jesus's day?
2. Do you agree that the crucifixion created a problem for the early Christian apologists to overcome?

35. Walters, *Rufus Jones Essential Writings*, 31.

3. Have you struggled with understanding the miracle stories?
4. Do you agree that a parallel was being drawn with Moses to legitimize Jesus?
5. What have you thought about atonement?
6. What is your overall reaction to this chapter?

5

The Human Being

To have a self, to be a self, is the greatest concession made to man, but at the same time it is eternity's demand upon him.

Soren Kierkegaard

What does it mean to be a human being, created in the very image of God? Much of that depends upon what one imagines about God. If one believes God is vengeful, focused on revenge against sinners to be meted on some future judgment day, they will have a very different view than an open Christian that believes in God as a ubiquitous, perfectly loving consciousness. Unlike God, human consciousness comes enveloped in a corporate body, at least initially, for the time we know as life on earth. This corporate body has its own needs in order to live, but should satisfying these needs be the only purpose for which humans exist? Kierkegaard, in the epigraph to this chapter, states that to have a self is God's concession to humanity. But this concession is not a gift without strings. These strings are what a human being makes of this gift. How will they respond to eternity's demand upon them. What will they struggle to become?

AN OPEN CHRISTIANITY AND EDEN

The Eden mythology of Genesis places the newly created man, Adam, and woman, Eve, in a utopian garden where, in innocence, all their needs were provided for. Then they took the leap and ate fruit from the tree of knowledge. God had forbidden them from eating this fruit and, as punishment for having done so, they were cast out of the garden and into a life where women bear children in pain and men toil to eat. This was the original sin. In the fourth and fifth centuries CE, Augustine wrote extensively about how Adam and Eve's original sin tainted all of humankind. The doctrine of original sin has been criticized for the potential harm it can do to a person's self-image and psychological well-being. Matthew Fox has argued against the doctrine and proposed it be replaced with *original blessing*. But even with all its shortcomings, original sin, in one form or another, is still predominant in today's Christian worship themes and liturgies.

Perhaps, the Genesis episode could be understood differently. What if we thought of Adam and Eve's expulsion not as God's punishment but as the turning point when humans transcended from a fully dependent state into an independent self, capable of self-determination. Think of it as God, like a mother robin, kicking these youngsters out of the nest and onto their own. Here, one is not born to sin but to become a blessing, with an opportunity for self-determination and potential for becoming a precise image of God. Kierkegaard's "call to discern eternity's demand"[1] is one's journey into self-discovery and self-determination. In still another essay, Kierkegaard warned that "one lives only once. If that is let slip, . . . it is eternally irremediable."[2] It is the task of the human, in his or her time allotted, to responsibly address this opportunity. This chapter recounts opportunities and responsibilities along this journey.

1. My paraphrase based on his writing "to be a self is the greatest concession made to man, but at the same time is eternity's demand upon him." Kierkegaard, *Kierkegaard Anthology*, 344.

2. Kierkegaard, *Kierkegaard Anthology*, 459.

BECOMING A PERSON

Before we consider such matters, perhaps we should recount how it all begins, how we become part of the human family. Our human journey starts when a father's sperm unites with a mother's egg to form a zygote that grows into an embryo, and then a formed child that is typically pushed out of the mother's womb and through her birth canal into the cosmos, all in the space of nine months. Birth is not an easy entry into the world, nor something taken lightly by the mother. The comedian Carol Burnett once explained to a male friend what it was like birthing a child. "It is like this, take your lower lip and firmly stretch it out." The friend said, "Well that's not so bad." The comedian said, "Now stretch it back over your head."[3] Enough said!

There is, of course, no agreement when, during this prebirth journey, the subject in question becomes a human. Some say at conception; others, when life is viable outside the womb; and still others, at first breath after birth itself. Our task is not to weigh in on this matter. But perhaps, we can all agree that life's journey begins when the child is expelled from a mother's womb.

After birth, the existential journey begins. Initially, this infant life is heavily dependent on others, which lessens with the right of passage from infancy into childhood. But even before this happens, the self has begun to form and express itself in various ways. Childhood is a time of wondrous imagination and a sense of endless possibility. During my wife's years teaching kindergarten, she would ask children if they could fly. Almost always, they said yes. She would have them stand on a small chair, flap their arms, and jump. Of course no one was able to fly. A small step into reality.

It is typical for young girls to dote over baby dolls, host imaginary tea parties, and dream of being ballerinas or princesses. Boys imagine being cowboys, play with trucks, and dream of becoming policemen or firemen. The point here is not to foster gender stereotypes or promote a rigid binary gender agenda but to illustrate the imaginative spirit of young children.

3. Socratic Method, "Carol Burnett."

Near the end of my first decade beyond the womb, I took on the persona of a young Indian brave. In character, I cut a branch from a wild cherry tree, skinned it with a knife, and with my wood-burning set, burned my imaginary name, Golden Arrow, onto it. Adding string, I fashioned a bow; other branches became my arrows. Not long after that, I was convinced that I could dig my way to China. I did find my way to China, but not until decades later and in a professional capacity, arriving via airplane. Childhood was a wonderful time of my life. But more importantly, it gave me a capacity for wonder and imagination that I maintain into my octogenarian years. During these early years, children gain greater agency and develop skills they will use throughout their life.

Childhood is followed by the adolescent years, a period of expanding agency and startling, sometimes uncertain, realities. Young men's and women's bodies mature. Girls' breasts develop, and menstruation begins. The boys' genitals enlarge and they may frequently experience unsolicited erections. Social groups form that may become cliques. Being part of an in-group often becomes paramount, influencing who or what one admires and, perhaps, mimics. It can determine outward appearances, such as hairstyle, facial hair for young men, and style of dress. Some may fall almost totally under this spell, while others, perhaps rejected or overlooked, become loners, antisocial, or suffer from social awkwardness. It is a confusing time of change and development of the social persona.

Then, all of a sudden, one is cast into adulthood. The parental umbrella loses much of its earlier control, protection, and guidance. One is confronted with forging their own way, draped in the exterior body of an adult human being. Adult maturation is not instantaneous, rather, it is the beginning of a lifetime of learning, experimenting, and experiencing. It is in adulthood that Kierkegaard's thoughts about self are most salient, with the realization that one has a self, and one can mostly make it what they want it to be. The essence of who I am and who I should become is paramount. The self is now responsible for what it becomes. God's concession of selfhood, as Kierkegaard put it, is now operable and eternity's demand is to be sought within the mystery of life.[4]

INTEGRITY

With existential questions now on the table, the response can be to capitulate to what others think one should be or, more hopefully, take responsibility and boldly strike out on one's own path. In our late twenties, my wife and I attended a marriage retreat. One of the exercises we did required magazines, tape, a paper bag, and scissors. We were given instructions to cut items from the magazines that illustrated how others thought of us and tape them on the outside of the bag. We were then asked to cut out items that illustrated who we believed ourselves to be and place them inside the bag. The lesson to be learned was that where our internal self and the external projection were aligned, we experienced integrity and wholeness. That is when one is on their way to becoming authentically human.

I, THOU, AND CREATION

Austrian Israeli philosopher Martin Buber has written about interacting with other humans as subjects, rather than as objects, in an I–Thou relationship.[5] His point is that we should take interest in others as fellow humans and not as things to be used or manipulated for personal gain. But we do take shortcuts and use others selfishly. In fact, we often treat Jesus this way. We noted this earlier, noting that Howard Thurman expressed this when he said he wanted to write about Jesus as a *religious subject* rather than a *religious object*. As subject, one invites Jesus and his essence into their life; as object, they use him for their own ends.

But, while we have evolved into the highest form of complex sentient beings with the ability to meet many of our individual

4. Kierkegaard, *Kierkegaard Anthology*, 344.

5. Buber, *I and Thou*.

needs, we also mustn't objectify the contribution that nonhuman sentient beings have made to our development and, today, contribute to our survival. Neil Shubin, in his book *Your Inner Fish*, traces the evolution of the human body from early aquatic fossils to its present complexity, noting that over hundreds of million years, primitive body parts adapted and were repurposed to become what they are today. Shubin writes, "We are not separate from the rest of the living world; we are part of it down to our bones, and . . . even our genes."[6] Shubin added that the DNA combination for developing arms, wrists, and digits is virtually identical in every creature that has limbs. While humans may be in a class by themselves with respect to their highly developed capacity for thought and consciousness, the architecture and development of their bodies is shared throughout the cosmos. But even pieced together with newly designed and repurposed parts, humans are far from self-sufficient.

NO PERSON AN ISLAND.

Professor Pamela Lyon of the University of Adelaide, a basal cognition scholar, has quipped that "if we start realizing that we have a whole lot more in common with the blades of grass and the bacteria in our stomachs—that we are related at a really, really deep level—it changes the entire paradigm of what it is to be a human being on this planet."[7] We take for granted and completely ignore the 100 trillion microbe cells living in our bodies, forming a cooperative inner ecosystem and carrying out tasks without which we would perish.[8] We ingest, host, and excrete these microbes in every moment of our lives. The cellular functioning of every living thing follows a similar pattern. Our physical bodies are not an island, nor are we totally unique; every living thing is a cousin, sibling, or distant generational parent to us. All complex forms of

6. Shubin, *Your Inner Fish*, 44.
7. Jacobsen, "Brains Are Not Required," para. 43.
8. Davenport et al., "Human Microbiome in Evolution."

life contain billions of cells containing deoxyribonucleic acid, or DNA, with its specific instructions defining a life, and mitochondrial DNA that powers life's responses. We share common DNA sequences with nearly all living entities, both plants and animals. We are one participant in the life of our ecosystem and sea of consciousness. We should treat not only our fellow human travelers as I–Thou subjects but also all life as valued subjects in the web of consciousness.

SELF AND ENVIRONMENT

We are indeed swimming in a sea of consciousness, rhythmically dancing to God's ubiquitous life-giving song of love and cooperation. But is this a gift in which no reciprocal action on our part is expected? Does eternity demand that we respect and participate in sustaining this space in which we live and breathe and have our being?

A common saying among people living in the mountains is "If you're lucky enough to live in the mountains, you are lucky enough!" Twenty years ago, my wife and I became lucky enough. We retired and relocated to a home in the mountains of Colorado. Living at the summit of Ute Pass 9,200 feet above sea level is not for everyone. For many, the altitude literally takes their breath away. But altitude is not the only thing that can take your breath away. Our aspen-treed property also has sweeping views of Pikes Peak, America's Mountain, which was the inspiration for Katharine Lee Bates composing "America the Beautiful."[9] Pikes Peak is just one of Colorado's fifty-eight "fourteeners," mountains with peaks over fourteen thousand feet above sea level. For that reason, Coloradans tend to take its relationship with nature seriously.

The Bible has little to say about our responsibilities toward the sentient ecosystem. While "earth" appears one thousand and twenty-six times in the Bible, including the Apocrypha, outside of

9. Gilder Lehrman Institute of American History, "America the Beautiful."

Genesis, it says little about our responsibility towards the ecosystem. Here is what it does say.

> God blessed them, and God said to them, Be fruitful and multiply and fill the earth and subdue it and have dominion over the fish of the sea and over the birds of the air and over every living thing that moves upon the earth.[10]

But this lacks clarity. How should we understand "subdue and have dominion"? Does it mean take from nature without regard to its renewal? Social ethicist Larry Rasmussen has written that we treat the earth like a slave, i.e., property to be bought, sold, and used indiscriminately for the benefit of the slaveholder—in this case, us.[11] Is this what is meant in the Genesis passage? Perhaps. Or perhaps, ecological issues just weren't an issue on the minds of the ancients at the time.

Biblical scholars believe that Genesis was finalized in the fifth century BCE.[12] The temple had been destroyed and their leadership taken into captivity. Exiled in Babylon, Israel's religious leaders' focus was on Israel's God, YHWH, especially with respect to Babylon's god, Mazda. They questioned why YHWH would permit this to happen to them. Was it because Mazda was much more powerful than YHWH? The narrative ultimately adopted was that they were experiencing the repercussions of deviating from God's covenant with Israel. I suspect ecological matters were far from their minds at this point.

At the time Genesis was written, the world's population was between one hundred million and two hundred million people.[13] Using the higher estimate, each person's share of the earth's volume was 1,295,000 cubic miles. It must have seemed limitless. Today, with 8.1 billion earthlings, each person's share of the earth's volume is less than 320 cubic miles. That is a factor of 4,050 times less than when Genesis was written. You can see where this is going. As

10. Gen 1:28.

11. Rasmussen, *Earth Honoring Faith*, 100.

12. Carr, *Formation*, 285–89.

13. McEvedy and Jones, *Atlas of World Population History*, 342–51.

the earth's population grows, its resources must serve more people every day. Further, the demands placed upon that shrinking space are growing as the amount of resources consumed per person accelerates. Will we reach a point when the earth's resources are insufficient to support human life?

While some resources are regenerative (i.e., able to replace themselves), the resources we extract for energy purposes—coal, oil, and natural gas—take millions of years to regenerate, and precious metals take millions to perhaps a billion years to replenish. For all practical purposes, these resources are nonrenewable. But this is only part of the picture. Today, we are polluting our atmosphere at a faster rate than our atmosphere can renew itself. Prior to 1850, negligible amounts of CO_2 were emitted into the world's atmosphere. Since then, the rise of industrialization and personal transportation has increasingly pumped greater amounts of CO_2 into the atmosphere, reaching billions of tons being pumped into the atmosphere since 1850. Further, the concentration of CO_2 and other gases are warming the planet. While in biblical times, ecological issues and environmental renewal were not an issue, today, the matter is becoming increasingly important. With 8.1 billion people and growing, sharing the same finite land, sea surface, and nonrenewable resources, we will reach a point when our finite resources are exhausted. Perhaps, it is another hundred years; perhaps, sooner. Humans are the only beings with the sentient consciousness that can proactively respond to this. And they must. It is an existential demand and responsibility of the human species.

One might convincingly argue that the world's resources belong to all the world's people and should be managed accordingly. But like so many things, this is infeasible. Countries differ in their richness of resources. More powerful countries exploit less powerful countries for control of resources. Within and across countries, individuals and corporations gain control of vast amounts of resources and profit enormously from their ownership. As a source of wealth, their motivation is to retain control and promote the exploitation of these resources at the expense of the development of renewable sources and the sustainability of earth's resources for all of humanity. Thus, God's gift has become a gift to only a very small sliver of humanity. Considering this, what does Micah's assertion to "do justice, love kindness, and walk humbly with God" imply for today? Answering that question is our human responsibility.

EARTH: A SUPREME COOPERATIVE OPEN SYSTEM

Today, our earthly habitat is indeed an amazingly unique and complex entity of sentient beings cooperatively working together for mutual survival, from the simplicity of flora providing oxygen for fauna's livelihood and fauna returning the favor with carbon dioxide for flora's survival, with insects pollinating plants to ensure their viability for their next generation to the mutual dependence of humans on microbes to sustain life. This ecosystem is an open system populated with open subsystems receiving and exchanging information and tasks to promote and sustain life. All that exists at any time is made up of repurposed material differentiated by their own DNA recipe. Creation has a love rhythm, and we must learn to dance with it and not block it out with our own deafness and dysfunctional noise. The created self of an open Christian, with heightened awareness of the pain and deterioration being inflicted upon our biosphere, appreciates both our dependance on and obligation to preserve its health and wellbeing by advocating for conservation, sustainable processes, and renewable forms of energy. As it was with the medieval mystic, poet, and Catholic friar Saint Francis, we should all become patrons of ecology and practice eco-communalism, expressing love toward self, neighbor, and biosphere. It may be the key to survival for all of us sentient beings. This is the open Christian's understanding of the personal and collective responsibility of the human family and what it means to be human.

THOUGHT EXERCISE

1. Does consciousness make sense as humanity's connection with God and all of creation?
2. Do you think it is time to retire the doctrine of original sin?
3. Is it a far stretch to see Adam and Eve's expulsion from Eden as a "kicking out of the nest"?
4. Have you witnessed times when Jesus was treated as an object? If so, explain.
5. Have you been aware of the interconnectedness of humans with all sentient beings?
6. Do you agree or disagree that protecting the environment is a Christian matter?

6

Source, Prototype, Works in Progress

True godliness does not turn men out of the world but enables them to live better in it and excites their endeavors to mend it.

William Penn

An open Christianity was presented as a reform and alternative to traditional Christianity in response to the past decades of people abandoning their Christian identity and the tepid involvement of many of those remaining Christian. Concurrently, belief in traditional Christian teachings has also declined. An open Christianity deconstructs the doctrines, dogmas, and creeds and metaphorically plumbs the depths of traditional Christianity's often supernatural expression. What is left are very basic statements regarding a belief about God and Jesus's relationship to both God and humanity at its current stage of development. Holding all things together is faith in the superordinate commandment to love God and neighbor as the only feasible path for creation's journey. God of an open Christianity is a ubiquitous, perfectly loving conscious *Source*. Having been created in this image, humans have the potential to become perfectly loving. Jesus is the *Source's* messenger and fully developed *human prototype* that has pioneered the way. Through his teaching and lived example, he has shown us what a fully evolved human being is like. You and I, and with a few exceptions, all who have preceded us and many who will follow are *works in progress*—that is, works in progress slowly evolving to become Christlike in full communion with God the Source. But only if we choose to do so. In chapter 5, human dependence and interdependent responsibility to respect and protect our ecosystem was highlighted. In this chapter, we will focus on the meaning and development of a proactive self in a world that needs mending.

SELF

Kierkegaard has warned us of the responsibility each person has for taking charge of fashioning the self in *Fear and Trembling*, which, by the way is, the name of another of his writings.[1] At times, the formation of self occurs in an existential crisis. It may be fueled by doubt, a crisis in faith, and events totally beyond one's agency. It is a time when one reaches deep into their soul for a resolution. John of the Cross called this a *dark night of the soul*.[2]

Around age thirty, I had an existential watershed. My grandkids would probably say they didn't know people went through that sort of thing in the horse and buggy days. And maybe they didn't, but by 1973, my wife and I had been married for ten years, and we had three sons, the oldest about to attend kindergarten. My career in corporate America was taking off. But I was nagged by questions. Is this career what I want for our family? Who am I and who do I want to become? It was during this period of my life that I was introduced to Kierkegaard and began to take seriously Kierkegaard's admonitions about selfhood. I began writing short essays containing thoughts that Kierkegaard's writings triggered. One essay was appropriately entitled "Who Am I?" During this time, Elaine and I had extensive and, perhaps, exhausting discussions about determining our future, often accompanied with a

1. Kierkegaard, *Kierkegaard Anthology*, 116.
2. John of the Cross, *Collected Works of St. John*, 353–465.

glass of chardonnay. The rest is history; I left the corporate world. Armed with the GI Bill and a graduate assistantship, I entered the doctoral program at Michigan State University and began a thirty-year academic career. I had found my way, and a way to realize my true self. Building a self involves developing new or employing old skill sets and defining or redefining appropriate roles. Goals are set and pursued consistent with one's values and psychological and physical needs. Once achieved, the soul flourishes. All seems well. But is this the end? While all of this is preparation for performing a useful role in society and with loved ones, is it the end? Or is it just a waypoint, the beginning of a challenging lifelong journey?

JESUS THE ROLE MODEL

The biblical account of Jesus's life follows the pattern we have been discussing. After his baptism by John, in which he experienced God's affirmation, Jesus went into the wilderness to fine tune who he was going to be and become. He had role models he could emulate. Religious people of his day set themselves apart from the general population. Those inhabiting the temple wore ornate costumes, pompously acted out rituals, and enjoyed privileged respect in society. Other religious folks were arrogant, assertive preachers or esteemed experts in the "law." And there was John, eating locusts and honey, baptizing in the Jordan, and, at great personal risk, speaking uncomfortable truth to power, for which he literally lost his head. Which of these roles would Jesus assume? Or would he uniquely create his own? He chose the path of nonconformity.

The Gospels tell us that in the wilderness, Jesus rejected taking shortcuts (e.g., supernaturalism). He rejected keeping a low profile for personal safety. He rejected the pursuit of political power, riches, and comforts that would come with them. Jesus then constructed a transcended self. Living among the people, he told stories and parables that insulted the hierarchies; he told the one without sin to throw the first stone; he broke with the culture that shunned the lepers, isolated women during their menstrual cycle, and challenged money changers in the temple. The greatest transcendental challenge came to Jesus in the Garden of Gethsemane. As we recounted earlier, as the inevitability and reality of his crucifixion became ever clearer, he prayed from the depth of his being, "My Father, if it is possible, may this cup be taken from me. Yet not as I will, but as you will."[3] Jesus's selfhood was fashioned in the wilderness, and he fulfilled this selfhood transcending his personal needs for the common good of humanity.

TRANSCENDENCE: THE FREEDOM FROM ME

We have noted that in the early 1970s, shortly before his death, Abraham Maslow revised his need structure and, among other things, added transcendence as the highest order human need. His notions about transcendence are captured in the following quote.

> Transcendence refers to the very highest and most inclusive or holistic levels of human consciousness, behaving and relating, as ends rather than means, to oneself, to significant others, to human beings in general, to other species, to nature, and to the cosmos.[4]

The nature of transcendence partners nicely with Buber's description of the *I–Thou relationship*, which is characterized by mutual respect and regard for others beyond oneself. Buber hinted, as did Maslow, that this concern beyond oneself might be extended beyond human-to-human relationships to the entire cosmos, i.e., to all sentient beings. For an open Christian, transcendence is not denying the self; rather, transcendence fulfills the self. With transcendence, one is unified with others and the common good for all sentient beings. In transcendence, the common good becomes a person's self-interest, one's ultimate concern. It is a blending of self, self-concern, and self-consciousness into the entire sea of loving sentient consciousness. It is the beginning of co-creating a new future with the ubiquitous, perfectly loving conscious Source

3. Matt 26:39.
4. Colagrossi, "7 Common Traits," para. 3.

mentoring the cosmos in pursuit of perfection. It is Jesus, the prototype that teaches and shows us the way.

Open Christianity eschews legalisms, dualities, and judgment and invites all of existence into one's awareness to become part of an open self. One where walls and borders that have been constructed to protect the faith's exclusive remedy for redeeming humans' sinfulness and isolated it from the world's other religions are dismantled, or made porous, to permit the self to experience the wholeness and unity of reality and experience the divine. The transcendent soul as an open system is aware of what is going on in the greater reality and welcomes, rather than fears or avoids, experiences. It is a recursive process of open learning and experiencing, leading to an expanded self. It is the path to becoming fully human.

Transcendence is something that can easily be misconstrued. It is not characterized by busy work and being run ragged. Rather, it is a thoughtful approach using discernment and selectivity. The transcendent Christian can say no! It is a common trope that "one must take care of themselves before they can care for others or care for the common good." It is true that one can become overwhelmed at times, especially if they take on more than they can accomplish or become embroiled in projects of questionable value. An open Christianity is interested in success and positive outcomes. It eschews wasting energy pursuing goals of doubtful benefit or objectives beyond one's capabilities to achieve. As John put it, "Let us love not in word or speech but in *deed and truth*."[5] An open Christianity promotes discernment, the process of assessing where pivotal improvements can be made in the public space and evaluating one's available time, skills, and energy that could successfully address an improvement. In an open Christianity, transcendence assesses injustice and unkindness in the common space and humbly assumes projects for which one has the capability to address. It becomes a path to freedom from self, freedom from *me*.

5. 1 John 3:18.

SOUL MAINTENANCE

Inevitably, one will overschedule their energy source. It is in these times an open Christian turns to *soul maintenance.* Mystic meditation is an effective practice for soul maintenance. It involves prayer that differs from the more common petitionary prayer in which God's intercession is requested. Mystical meditation asks nothing from God. Rather, in quietude, one empties the mind of thought and enters the present moment, in waiting, to experience the unity of reality and the essence of God. In mystic meditation, one opens the mind to the cosmos rather than imposing a circumscribed self upon it. In mystical meditation, thought comes to you and you dissolve into it. And with it comes a peacefulness and a unity with God as a healing wave of love passes through the sea of consciousness, sentient life, and yourself. Entering mystical meditation is not just a respite; it is also a time when God can whisper thoughts of encouragement and inspiration. It brings one closer to the realization of God's presence while unifying the self with that presence and all sentient life. This form of prayer has the potential to soothe the soul and prepare the mind and body for a Christlike existence of peace, love, and healing in the world.

KAUFMAN'S COMMANDMENTS

In *Face of Mystery*, Gordon Kaufman wrote that human beings overall have three basic mandates. They are to act, to act morally, and to act ethically.[6] Human beings differ from all other living beings in that they have the imagination and ability to define themselves and the agency to implement that identity. Humans, unlike other sentient beings, can individually and collectively develop sophisticated strategies and implement actions to meet their various needs, and not only escape unpleasant or threatening environments but can literally change their environment to avoid future threats to survival. They can till the ground and plant crops to stabilize their food supply. They can dam rivers and streams to

6. Kaufman, *Face of Mystery*, 194–206.

create reservoirs to offset drought. They can cooperate to create institutions for their defense, education, and healing. This gift of self-determination places an obligation on humans to act and not merely be passive travelers through time and space. Kaufman's first mandate is to act.

One's actions should be moral. Cultures and societies, through time, adopt "acceptable" behaviors. These behaviors express values that support and maintain the community and promote societal cohesion. Shared values give the community functionality, common purpose, and shared responsibilities. Kaufman argues that we should act within the moral framework of values and accepted practices of our communities to preserve and strengthen unity and effectiveness. Kaufman's second mandate is to act morally.

Kaufman's third mandate is to act ethically. Morality and ethics are often conflated. Kaufman distinguishes between them. For Kaufman, while morality consists of long-standing values and behaviors a community or society adopts over time, ethics is the critique of those values and behaviors. Ethical inquiry assesses the consistency of moral behaviors with values over and against higher principled values. While morals are historically derived and foster stability, ethical behavior is disruptive, challenging communities to be more compassionate and just. Ethical critique of morality has costs, sometimes steep cost. To engage ethical critique, one must be willing to entertain those costs. Examples of the costs are abundant. The United States fought a civil war over the matter of slavery. Critiques of racial segregation of the 1950s and 1960s led to civil unrest and violence. Protesters were beaten and some murdered. Riots broke out in cities and national guardsmen were deployed to regain calm. Political assassinations occurred, beginning in 1963 with the murder of President Kennedy, followed five years later by the murder of his brother Robert and the great civil rights martyr Martin Luther King Jr. Ethical critique is not for the faint of heart!

KAUFMAN AND OPEN CHRISTIANITY

The commandment to act is simply a challenge to implement or act out our selfhood. An open Christian is challenged to an outward awareness of opportunities to act in love towards one's neighbor and all of creation. It calls upon awareness of the fabric or interconnected web of humanity, of which we are all a part, and calls on us to act in ways that strengthen the web and heal tears in the fabric. It acts and speaks against simplistic dichotomies that separate and discriminate against fellow travelers as good or evil, in-group or out-group. The open Christian seeks to clarify differences in behaviors, policies, and goals but refrains from name calling, artificial classifying, and destructive assumptions. An open Christian would strive to act in transcendence, reaching beyond self-interest to serve the church community and society at large. In such striving, one must develop a *thick skin* to avoid vindictively acting out in retribution, but also, the *thin skin sensitivity* to recognize communal hurt and injustice.

An open Christian, like all people, seeks to act within the bounds of the moral fabric of the society in which they live. But in doing so, an open Christian avoids demagoguery, using morality as platform for self-aggrandizement. Matthew warns in chapter 6 of his Gospel, "Beware of practicing your righteousness before others in order to be seen by them . . . whenever you give alms, do not sound a trumpet before you, as the hypocrites do in the synagogues and in the streets, so that they may be praised by others."[7]

Ethical action goes beyond acting morally, for which the open Christian has a call. An open Christian must challenge accepted moral guidelines in society as well as in Christianity. An open Christian is wary of *concrete* admonitions found in Scripture. Some passages are no longer relevant, such as the obvious example in Num 15, where a man is observed collecting sticks on the Sabbath and "the LORD said to Moses, 'The man shall be put to death; all the congregation shall stone him outside the camp.'"[8]

7. Matt 6:1.

8. Num 15:32–36.

Scripture was written when science was at a much earlier stage of development, when the cosmos was thought to exist in three tiers, with heaven located just above the earth, and illness was caused by malevolent spirits rather than germs and viruses. Abstract passages in Scripture have greater interpretative flexibility and are adaptable to changing reality. They are more durable and able to stand the test of time. This is especially true in a time when change comes at an increasingly fast pace, as it has since the Enlightenment. An open Christian challenges Scripture interpretation with respect to how it promotes and sustains love of God and neighbor.

Ethical critique is, by nature, transcendental behavior. The costs and risks of ethical critique are clear from the lives of Jesus, the Apostles, Perpetua and Felicity, Joan of Arc, Jan van Essen and Hendrik Vos, and more recently, Dietrich Bonhoeffer, Martin Luther King Jr., and Saint Oscar Romero. In an open Christianity, transcendent ethical critique enhances collective justice and is offered in love and humility. It is the pathway to becoming fully human, exemplified by Jesus of Nazareth.

In *The Sea of Faith*, Don Cupitt wrote "a person believes in God if the idea of God does some real work and plays a constitutive part in his thinking and in shaping his way of life."[9] That is the first existential task of the open Christian. Cupitt further wrote, "A religious act . . . has to be done for its own sake and because it is intrinsically good to do it, and not for the sake of some kind of subsequent pay-off."[10] That pertains to the second existential task of the open Christian, which is to transcend the self to pursue what is right for the common good and the greater sentient web of consciousness and life, which then, in Cupitt's words, is "the way of responding to and shaping life and giving ultimate meaning and value to life."[11]

Stated somewhat differently, the first existential task of the open Christian is to establish a self that is congruent with the two greatest commandments of the Christian religion, to love God and

9. Cupitt, *Sea of Faith*, 247.

10. Cupitt, *Sea of Faith*, 36.

11. Cupitt, *Sea of Faith*, 36.

neighbor. To fulfill this self, one also needs to move beyond merely satisfying one's internal needs to the second existential task of the open Christian. This is to strive for transcendence. It means moving beyond self, to adopt as a person's self-interest the interests of the common good. At times, that means acting morally; at other times, acting ethically; but clearly, acting—acting out one's core values. Seeking the greater common good, not personal salvation in an afterlife, is the ultimate objective of the Christian enterprise. An open Christianity believes that success in this matter is *personal salvation*. Further, it is the pathway to communal salvation, the keys to opening the doors to Jesus's *kingdom*. In brief, the existential challenge is to step outside the tyranny of self-absorption to achieve a greater uber-self, whose joy is found beyond self-aggrandizement and self-satisfaction, finding joy and fulfillment in serving the greater good. This is what it means to be fully human, fully alive. In the early centuries of the church, St. Irenaeus, Bishop of Lyon, put it this way: "The glory of God is a human being fully alive; and to be alive consists in beholding God."[12] Just as Paul is reported in Acts 17 to have said to the Athenians, it is in God that "we live and move and have our being."[13]

THOUGHT EXERCISES

1. Some people believe that God has a plan for their life. Is the human existential task to discern God's plan for them or to enter mystical contemplation for self-determination?
2. What role does Christian teaching play in a person's self-determination?
3. How does mystical contemplation compare to traditional prayer?

12. Irenaeus, *Against Heresies*, 4.20.7.

13. Acts 17:28.

4. Kaufman draws a distinction between moral behavior and ethical behavior. What examples can you think of that fit into this framework?
5. How would you describe the difference between a transactional Christianity and a transcendent Christianity?
6. Are there new insights in this chapter that changes your perspective on being Christian? If so, what are they?

PART 3

Practical Matters

7

Open Christianity and Christian Nationalism

Those who are in great fear are so intent on their own passion that they pay no attention to the suffering of others.

Thomas Aquinas

A long-standing Christian movement in the United States has been based on the understanding that at its founding, the United States was a Christian nation. The movement has waxed and waned over time and is now experiencing a resurgence. One of the more extreme forms of this is the charismatic movement known as the New Apostolic Reformation, which seeks to replace the constitutionally grounded American democracy with autocracy ruled by God, or at least by those who believe they know God's desires. It doesn't require much imagination to see where this would lead. Christian nationalism is a far cry from the reform called for in chapter 1. It is not, in any stretch of the mind, compatible with an open Christianity.

For many Christians, the argument that the United States was founded as a Christian nation makes a lot of sense. After all, the country had its beginnings with puritans and other religious groups escaping persecution in their homelands. The country's foundation documents guarantee freedom for all its citizens. It has become the greatest, most powerful and prosperous nation on earth, at least as Americans see it, and there is ample evidence to support this notion. Some Christians believe that all of this is due to God's favor, that the United States is the new Israel, and its citizens are God's chosen people. Further, the Gospel of Matthew calls us to "go therefore and make disciples of all nations, baptizing them in the name of the Father and of the Son and of the Holy Spirit."[1] What better way to do this than with the backing of the most powerful nation on earth. So why not boldly make the case and declare the United States a Christian nation?

Many years ago, when I was still in my twenties, my wife and I attended a church retreat. A speaker from South Africa spoke at the event, and as part of his presentation, he explained that in his younger years, he believed his country's citizens, South Africans, were God's chosen people. I remember being astounded by this. How could he have thought so? Then I realized the irony in all of this. God doesn't pick favorites. Indeed, "God is love"[2] and "makes his sun rise on the evil and on the good and sends rain on the righteous and on the unrighteous."[3]

The idea of Christian nationalism is as old as the founding of the earliest colonies on our shores. Philip Gorski and Samuel Perry trace the evolution of today's Christian nationalism from its roots in 1690 to the version being trumpeted by Donald Trump's followers today. Gorski and Perry describe Christian nationalism as being based on a deep mythical story, whose main theme is as follows.

> America was founded as a Christian nation by (white) men who were "traditional" Christians, who based the nation's founding documents on "Christian principles." The United States is blessed by God, which is why it has been so successful; and the nation has a special role to play in God's plan for humanity. But these blessings are

1. Matt 28:19.
2. 1 John 4:8.
3. Matt 5:45.

> threatened by cultural degradation from "un-American" influences both inside and outside our borders.[4]

In Christian Nationalism, the US Constitution takes on sacramental overtones. God has selected the United States to be special among nations and that it is being threatened by adversaries within the country, namely, progressives who they denigrate as radicals, communists, and godless socialists. Immigrants coming across our borders are seen as subverting our God-given American values. According to Gorski and Perry, Christian nationalists promote freedom for *their kind* and support violence when necessary to maintain their position in the social order. They further argue that Christian nationalism is not a conservative movement as many think; rather, it is a *reactionary* movement. It does not seek to preserve the status quo. Rather, it seeks to destroy the status quo and return to a mythical past, to *make America great again.*[5] But it is a past that never was.

In chapter 1, a case was made for reforming Christianity. But Christian nationalists do not seek reform; they seek a throwback to something that never existed. It is folly at best, and it is dangerous. Our founding documents, including the Declaration of Independence, declare all men are created equal. The assertion that "all men are created equal" was repeated by Lincoln in his address at Gettysburg.[6] The us of the masculine "all men" is clearly an artifact of the genre and custom of the day and should not be a distraction. All men means just as it says. It does not say all Christian men. The idea that Christians hold a special place in the United States is merely wishful thinking by those who might want to use a privileged position to rule the country.

Gorski and Perry devised a seven-question scale[7] to determine the extent a person subscribed to Christian nationalist

4. Gorski and Perry, *Flag and the Cross*, loc. 153.

5. Gorski and Perry, *Flag and the Cross*, loc. 1589.

6. Lincoln, "Gettysburg Address."

7. The scale items were 1) "I consider founding documents like the Declaration of Independence and the US Constitution to be divinely inspired," 2) "The success of the United States is part of God's plan," 3) "The federal government

ideology. Question 5 (see footnote) addressing separation of church and state was scored in reverse order. The higher total score, the stronger one's adherence to Christian Nationalist ideology. Their research showed that the higher a person scored on the Christian Nationalists scale, the more that White Christian nationalists subscribed to the following beliefs or actions:

- Christians will experience a lot of discrimination in the next year.
- It is too easy to vote in the US.
- BLM[8] and Antifa were in the crowd and started the violence at the Capitol on January 6, 2020.
- Violence is acceptable if the situation calls for it.
- They have more faith in Trump than the medical profession, the CDC, or scientists during the COVID-19 epidemic.
- Immigration should be stopped to protect American jobs.
- They oppose removing Confederate monuments and statues.
- They believe in a literal Armageddon and rapture.
- They are significantly less informed on American political history than those less inclined toward Christian nationalism.

In another study throughout 2023, the Public Religion Research Institute (PRRI), in cooperation with the Brookings Institution, gathered survey information from twenty-two thousand American adults as part of its *American Values Atlas*. In PRRI's study, subjects were presented with the following five statements:[9]

---

should declare the United States a Christian nation," 4) "The federal government should advocate Christian values," 5) "The federal government should enforce a strict separation of church and state," 6) "The federal government should allow the display of religious symbols in public spaces," and 7) "The federal government should allow prayer in public schools." Gorski and Perry, *Flag and the Cross*, loc. 314.

8. Black Lives Matter.

9. PRRI, "Christian Nation?," 33.

- "The U.S. government should declare America a Christian nation."
- "U.S. laws should be based on Christian values."
- "If the U.S. moves away from our Christian foundations, we will not have a country anymore."
- "Being Christian is an important part of being truly American."
- "God has called Christians to exercise dominion over all areas of American society."

Subjects scored zero if they disagreed with a statement and one if they agreed with it. The sample was then subdivided into four groups based upon their average score.

- Christian Nationalism Adherents (Score 0.75–1)
- Christian Nationalism Sympathizers (Score 0.5–0.74)
- Christian Nationalism Skeptics (Score 0.01–0.49)
- Christian Nationalism Rejecters (Score 0)

The study's results indicated that 10 percent of their subjects were Christian nationalist adherents and that another 20 percent were sympathizers, while 67 percent were either skeptics (37 percent) or rejecters (30 percent). Three percent of subjects did not provide an answer or did not have an opinion.

The PRRI study found the following.

- Christian nationalism has its greatest following among White Evangelical Christians.
- While evangelicals are five times as likely to be adherents as non-evangelical Christians, Christian nationalism is positively related to church attendance across all Christian groups.
- Christian nationalism is closely correlated with Republican politics and favorable views of Donald Trump.
- Christian nationalism is unrelated to gender but increases with age.

- Rejection of Christian nationalism increases with each level of additional education.
- Fifty-four percent of Republicans are adherents or sympathizers; 15 percent of democrats are adherents or sympathizers.
- Seventy-nine percent of adherents and sympathizers trust far-right news outlets.
- Sixty-nine percent of adherents and 51 percent of sympathizers agree that the man is the head of a household and a woman must submit to his leadership, while 33 percent of all Americans agree with this.
- While 16 percent of Americans in the study think the country is so far off track that political violence may be required to right things, the percentage jumps to 40 percent for Christian nationalist adherents.

Mark Shea believes that the affinity toward Christian nationalism among evangelicals stems from conservative Christians feeling threatened by "secularism" and see Christian nationalism as a defense against it.[10] Many biblical literalists still hold that women should take a back seat to the leadership of men in church and at home at least, if not in all of society. Yet the advances of women outside of helping roles, such as nursing and teaching, like fulfilling leadership positions in business, law, government, military, and even many churches does not sit well with many conservative Christians. Factors such as liberal churches ordaining homosexual clergy, marrying gay couples, and women taking prominent leadership roles in the military and government represent decay in society to many fundamentalists, rather than enlightened progress. The gender identification issue leaves many befuddled and even many *occasional* Christians in sympathy with fundamentalists' viewpoints. So, what is wrong with government declaring the United States a Christian nation? Christians still are the majority religion, so the majority should rule. Right?

10. Shea, "Dangers of Christian Nationalism."

Many things are wrong with this position. First, our founding documents do not just provide for majority rule; they also provide protection for minorities. But, perhaps more importantly, we have centuries of experience of what can go wrong when Christianity is aligned with political power. It will inevitability lead to powerful individuals projecting their own needs and desires onto God, claiming it is God's will and pursuing their goals under the banner of God. The abuse began in ancient Rome once Christianity became legitimized in the fourth century. At that time, the centuries-long saga of Christians killing or maiming Christian *heretics* began. In the middles ages, with the church aligned with political power, countless nonconformers were drowned, beheaded, burned at the stake and/or tortured. Over centuries, when the church had political might, it tortured and murdered Jews; conquistadors mutilated, slaughtered, and enslaved native peoples; and in our country, Christians, in good conscious, murdered defenseless Native American women, children, and elderly. It is noteworthy that the justification for the slavery industry and the institution of *Jim Crow* were most prevalent in a region of our country known as the *Bible belt.* A unifying of church and state would undoubtedly lead to an unmitigated hell for many of our friends, neighbors, and fellow travelers.

Further, if the United States were to be declared a Christian nation, whose Christianity would be in charge? The progressives? Unlikely. The moderates? Also, unlikely. It would be the evangelicals, charismatics, and fundamentalists, the ones most aligned with Christian nationalism. How long would it take those in charge for their philosophy to reflect *ends justifying the means*, exchanging fiat for love? How long would it take for power-hungry men to claim they represent the will to God and, as a result, make America a living hell? So, what position would an open Christianity take regarding Christian nationalism?

AN OPEN CHRISTIANITY PERSPECTIVE

Christian nationalism is unchristian. In an open Christianity, God inspires and encourages, evolving all of humanity toward higher unity and wholeness. Christian nationalism perpetuates a closed system, ridged rules, and privilege primarily for White American men. Christian nationalism draws upon proof-texting, whereby Bible passages are taken out of context and used to support their movement. An open Christianity uses the two greatest commandments of loving God and neighbor as the pinnacle of Scripture, within which all other Scripture and initiatives are measured.

In the desert, Jesus eschewed all shortcuts to implement his ministry. No self-serving abuse of power, no abusive use of God, no supernaturalism, and most notably, no use of worldly power to undergird his ministry. When he sent his disciples out among the people, as recorded in Matthew, he sent them as sheep among the wolves, not with armed guards or pouches of money but as humble faithful servants. In Matt 5, Jesus talks about the humble, not the powerful, being the people of God.

Jesus gives example after example of "who is my neighbor," from the good samaritan, to the prodigal son, to the leper, to the hemorrhaging woman, to the blind, to the adulteress, and so on. Christian nationalism answers the question "Who is my neighbor?" with "My neighbor is all those just like me!" Samaritans need not apply! Jesus said his kingdom is not of this world, meaning that it had no geographic boundaries, no power center, no structure other than love, kindness, and unity. The kingdom is not a group of elites made up of insiders that are in the know, while all others are sons and daughters of Satan. In an open Christianity, Jesus's kingdom does not seek to separate us into haves and have-nots or to dominate an *out-of-favor* group. Rather, the kingdom seeks to unify with love. Justifying vengeance as being an agent of God can be an exhilarating self-reinforcing behavior, one that is all-consuming. But, it is a false transcendence that is nothing more than making oneself a god over others judged less worthy.

Christian nationalism is simply anti-Jesus, anti-Christian, counterproductive, and certainly counter to an open Christianity

THOUGHT EXERCISES

1. Do you believe the United States is a Christian nation? Explain.
2. What influence, if any, should Christianity have on law making in the US?
3. Do you think Christian nationalism is a threat to the US and beyond?
4. What should be the church's role with respect to Christian nationalism?
5. If somehow Christian nationalism became predominate, whose version of Christianity would likely prevail?
6. What do you think is the best way to counter Christian nationalism?

8

Advancing an Open Christian Expression

Nor does anyone pour new wine into used wineskins.

MARK 2:22

AN OPEN CHRISTIANITY CAN spark new understanding and a renewed commitment for an individual exhausted by supernaturalism and medieval logic still prevalent in most of our current worship and study groups. It can release the follower from exposure to confusing and conflicting concepts of God still circulated from our pulpits and talked about in our study groups for all ages. In an open Christianity, with its understanding of God as the ubiquitous, loving consciousness mentoring the cosmos, characterization of God as vengeful, judgmental, controlling, withdrawn, and/or transactional can be relegated to the annals of history. Further, the role of Jesus is clearly delineated and the challenge for humans to become fully human in the image of God is understood as the transcendental, existential challenge for humans both individually and collectively. But can this be achieved in today's Christianity? With its comfortable patterns of worship not dissimilar to what it was half a century ago and with congregants that, to be frank, since middle school years, have too often been pacified rather than theologically challenged? I believe today's churches would benefit, as I have written earlier, from greater courage in our pulpits and increasing curiosity in our pews. An open Christian church could provide the reform needed to again put adventure in the Christian journey. But what would this look like? An open Christian community thrives in creative expression. In this chapter, we will entertain aspects of an open Christianity without becoming dogmatic or overly prescriptive. We will review several open Christian perspectives, construct sample vision and mission statements, and suggest some practical matters that may be pursued in an open Christian community. But first, a word of caution.

NEW WINE AND OLD WINESKINS

Introducing open Christianity into an existing congregation is analogous to the New Testament parable of pouring new wine into old wineskins. Something must give or the wineskin will burst. Can a church in the traditional mold become an open Christian church? The answer is maybe, but not without birthing pains. Jesus warned in the first century CE that "no one after drinking old wine desires new wine but says, the old is good."[1] Can the partakers of the old wine learn to imbibe the new? My personal experience is probably not, at least not without some degree of pain and disruption. As an example, eighteen years ago, I began a progressive adult class in a traditional congregation, offering the new wine of progressive Christian authors. While the class took hold and, for that matter, still meets on Sunday mornings, the congregational drinkers satisfied with the old wine looked at us with disdain and distress. We were accused of being in bed with Lucifer. We still exist, but all these years later, we remain theological outsiders separate from the congregation's mainstream. Can the new wine of an open Christianity be poured into the old wineskin of today's church?

1. Matt 9:17; Mark 2:22; Luke 5:37–39.

Even moderately introducing new wine into the old wineskins can lead to strife in the pews. Recently, United Methodists chose new wine by renouncing gay and lesbian sexual practice as being incompatible with Christian teaching, ordaining openly gay and lesbian clergy, and condoning same-sex marriage. It was the abandonment of positions that the church held since its formation in 1968. The old wineskin burst. Many congregations accepted and supported the change, but others disaffiliated from the denomination and formed the Global Methodist Church, an alternative upstart Methodist denomination. Other, often larger, congregations disaffiliated, becoming independent Methodist churches. University Methodist Church in San Antonio, a church my wife and I were instrumental in its launching decades ago, has recently taken this route.

The United Methodists were just the latest to make such a move. The United Church of Christ, Episcopal Church, Presbyterian Church USA, Alliance of Baptists, Disciples of Christ, and Evangelical Lutheran Church of American experienced serious losses of membership and suffered vile criticism when they took a similar path earlier. Individual clergy, like the late Episcopal Bishop John Shelby Spong, an avid proponent of progressive theological reform, are reported to have experienced frequent death threats.[2] Reform is not for the timid, and initiatives are typically met with resistance, fear, and backlash—sometimes, even with the potential for violence.

The last few decades of Christian decline suggests that not all Christians savor the old wine. I believe there is a critical mass of Christians, or would-be Christians, hungering for a new wine that is appropriate for our time. Leadership may be able to introduce it into traditional churches. But the ride will be rough, accusations will be made, and feelings will be hurt. Members will leave. Churches may even fail before they have a chance to succeed. It will be best for churches bent on reform to act early, accepting the departure of friends and fellow congregants unable to adapt. It will be painful, but doing so can preclude reaching a later stage,

2. Griffin, "My Deconstruction Heroes."

when the loss of each additional member imperils the church's very existence. An easier and less painful path is to plant a new church. Whether a new church plant or conversion of an existing congregation, what would it look like?

OPEN CHRISTIAN PERSPECTIVES

Open Christianity is not intended to be a new denomination adding to the multitude of existing denominations, cults, and churches. Rather, it encompasses a set of perspectives that an open Christian community would promote and facilitate. Following are six perspectives that would be appropriate in an open Christian community.

An Open System

An open Christianity has leaky borders, welcoming and learning from all human experience. Its holistic grounding avoids artificial dichotomies, such as sacred/secular, present life/afterlife, good/evil. It maintains a nuanced understanding of reality, enriched by science, art, poetry, and other world and indigenous religious teachings. Within this framework, the open systems perspective welcomes valid learning opportunities, promoting a more loving and caring humanity.

Outcomes Oriented

An open Christianity minimizes the presence of beliefs, creedal statements, and doctrines as litmus tests for being Christian. It values orthopraxy (right practice) over orthodoxy (right beliefs). Rather, Christian commitment is a matter of intention and follow-up behavior. Promoting loving behavior is the objective. Further, those loving behaviors are not to be limited to one's own kind or within one's own comfort zone. Rather, love is extended beyond comfort zones.

Present Focus

An open Christianity operates in the *here and now*, de-emphasizing hypothetical postmortem beliefs. Its interest is in furthering Jesus's notion of the kingdom, a society where love overcomes distrust and dissension.

Mysticism, Yes; Supernaturalism, No

An open Christianity understands God as a perfectly loving consciousness within, among, and beyond us, evolving the cosmos and mentoring humanity toward becoming more fully human, thus reflecting God's very image. This mystical presence exists perfectly within the boundaries of the naturally evolved cosmos.

Salvation

Open Christianity understands salvation as applicable to both an individual and collectively to the human family. For an individual, it is the path to transcendence where achievement of the common good supersedes striving for self-aggrandizement. It is the denying of self, taking up our challenges, collectively building a society fashioned in love and modeled after the kingdom as Jesus imagined it.

Interconnectedness

An open Christian community appreciates humanity's immense agency to act in and on our environment. It appreciates that we exist in a sea of interdependent sentient consciousness, with which we have a mutual responsibility to honor, respect, and protect. Through an all-encompassing love, an open Christian church supports ecological initiatives, seeks to better understand how to preserve our environment, and celebrates reality's interconnectedness.

STRATEGIC MATTERS: VISION AND MISSION

Without a thoughtfully strategic vision, an open Christian community will struggle and potentially fail. That means constructing a vision statement that can unify the community's direction and supporting activities. Most church communities are ill-equipped to develop an effective, directional, and motivational overall vision statement. Therefore, we shall take a few moments to flesh out this matter.

A vision statement is an account of a desired state of future affairs that an organization seeks to promote. Vision statements too often fall prey to lengthy and flowery acts of wordsmithery, resulting in a collection of empty platitudes. But the best ones are aspirational and succinct. Being aspirational means that they are not easily, and perhaps never, achieved. But one might ask, "Isn't that just blue-sky projection?" What is its value if it is never achieved? Consider Jesus's vision of what he called the kingdom. It was a worthy aspiration, but two thousand years later, it is still a work in progress. Yet, it still provides inspirational direction. That is the value of a carefully thought-through vision statement, i.e., its ability to provide direction for the community. One might think of it as a guiding star, like that leading the wise men to Bethlehem. The vision begins to narrow down the parameters for an organization's mission, yet leaves plenty of wiggle room for adjustment.

Effective vision statements are succinct and capture the imagination. They must also easily be called to mind. Long, flowery visions can inspire, but they are easily forgotten and often put on a shelf, only to be brought out for discussion and possible revision at next year's planning session. Another common error is limiting the vision within church walls. Examples are "Our congregation fully demonstrating the love of Jesus," or "A family with a place for everyone," or perhaps, "A congregation living out the gospel." These are all nicely succinct and somewhat inspirational statements. They are possibly achievable, but are they really worthy of honoring the person who is the foundation of our faith and died on a Roman cross? An open Christian community should aspire for more than what can be accomplished within church walls.

An open Christian vision should aspire to achieving outcomes beyond its church walls. I worked with a church task force on a vision statement a short time ago. For illustration purposes, I will share the vision statement that this task force created. Obviously, this is just an example, not one to be simply copied. The task force creates value by tailoring the vision to their own community's particular situation as well as becoming advocates for the vision motivated by their participation in the statement's development. In the present example, the task force wished to pursue an aspirational direction that they realized they would never fully achieve. Their statement follows.

A future where peace is found and God's love prevails.

This statement is succinct and clearly aspirational. It will obviously not be achieved any time soon. Yet, it is a statement that inspires commitment, is consistent with prioritizing loving God and neighbor, and provides direction. It is also a vision for life beyond the church's walls.

While a vision statement provides broad direction, it is generally insufficient for developing the concrete objectives and plans that are needed to move the community forward. An organization's mission fulfills that intermediate step between the vision statement and subsequent goal setting. Experience has shown that church missions frequently fall prey to being lengthy, containing every aspiration or desire the church administrators have ever had. Effective mission statements focus attention. Just as with vision statements, less is preferred to more. A concise statement is much more readily remembered, easily communicated, and pursued. It will efficiently act as the framework for establishing the church's future goals and strategies. The following is an example of a mission statement appropriate for an open Christian congregation. It also came from the task force mentioned above.

Love unconditionally, grow spiritually, and serve faithfully.

Notice, again, the succinctness of the statement and how it can support and advance the vision. The two work as hand in glove. These are two examples that can set the tone for vision and mission development. As noted earlier, the most effective statements are ones that are devised by those who are actually going to pursue the vision and implement the mission.

Once vision and mission statements are drafted, the next steps are to develop appropriate goals, implementation plans, and assessment methods. Goal setting, implementation plans, and assessment methods must be plausible taking into consideration the open Christian community's financial resources, physical facilities, and other vital resources. Of particular importance is the consideration of the skill set, passion level, and experience of leadership and planning participants. When these steps have been completed, the field is open for mission pursuit and progress being made toward vision attainment.

PRACTICAL MATTERS FOR AN OPEN CHRISTIAN CHURCH

It is recognized that open Christian communities will differ considerably from location to location. The weaving of open Christian perspectives into the community's operations and activities will take different routes and originate from different styles of creative expression. Following are open Christian initiatives that can be woven into a community either at its founding or more gradually over time. Some of these are already practiced or found in contemporary churches. The practical matters that follow may be appropriate for worship services, age-appropriate study groups, and administrative meetings.

Ancient Writings

Christianity's earliest Scriptures were articulated about thirty-five hundred years ago, and its latest, two thousand years ago. Many of the foundational doctrines and creeds were formulated sixteen hundred years ago while some current circulating theories (e.g., substitutionary atonement) were constructed over centuries, with today's most prevalent version being drafted in medieval times. While this is obvious, it is important to emphasize that ideas that find their way into Christian literature are not independent of the matrix in which they are formed. While it is true that some writings are eternally valid as they appear, many are time and culture sensitive, a reflection of the state of knowledge and cultural challenges of the time in which they were written. Consequently, presenting these readings in worship or study groups should never be done without explaining the matrix of concerns and motivations that triggered them to be written. This especially applies to Scripture readings but also to various liturgies and creeds that might be included in worship or study.

Mysticism

The foundational understanding of God as the ubiquitous, loving consciousness mentoring the cosmos has a deeply mystical component. In group meetings, whether it be worship, study session, or church administration, a brief moment of silence, perhaps accompanied by a breathing exercise or interlaced with calming statements at the start, can be beneficial. It can bring people to a state of calmness for entering the mystic presence and union with ubiquitous loving consciousness.

Holistic Context

An open Christian community emphasizes the unity and interdependencies of creation. Liturgies, hymns, and teachings should strive to emphasize this by avoiding dualisms that separate and divide reality into categories. With a ubiquitous loving deity, all of reality is sacred. While circumstances for some can create a living hell at times, it is a shared loving presence that can bring healing. Wisdom, beauty, and insight found in contemporary music, poetry, and literature are appropriate triggers for reflection and should be included in an open Christian community's worship and study.

Language

Words convey meaning that sometimes carry excess baggage. People who have been hurt by the church or have turned away for other reasons are often turned off by words and phrases common in Christian worship and study. They mentally space out or react negatively when they cross them. In still other cases, words convey meanings that today have lost their original meaning and are misunderstood.[3] Leadership's sensitivity to this matter and avoidance of these words and phrases can compensate for potential damage by substituting more contemporary expressions for what these words are meant to convey. A few examples of words to avoid or clarify are "repent," "salvation" or "saved," "righteousness," "sin," and "redeemer" or "redemption." Similarly, phrases such as "second coming" and comments like "have a blessed day" or being asked in a public space to pray, while well-intentioned, can stir negative responses derived from unfortunate experiences suffered when previously hearing these expressions. Other Christian terminology should be avoided if it leads to exclusiveness and enhances separateness. Concepts such as *being saved* divide people into saved and unsaved groups. Also, words that have meaning only for the initiated or in-group should be minimized and avoided. *Born again* could fall into this category. In short, words that act as de facto secret handshakes should not be part of open Christian dialogue.

Music, Responsive Readings, and Alternative Languages

Music is an important part of a worship service, and most services contain some responsive readings. The recommendation is that

3. For more extensive coverage, see Borg, *Speaking Christian*.

music should be supportive of open Christian themes, which generally means avoiding militaristic and fundamentalist themes. Similar to earlier recommendations, contemporary and popular music outside the Christian genre that carries an appropriate message for the service's theme should be a candidate for inclusion. Readings from non-Christian and contemporary sources can also enhance the message of a worship service or study session while supporting a theme of human unity. The insertion of other languages in part or whole within readings, responses, or music can help broaden minds and build bridges across divides in God's creation.

Doctrine

An open Christian church is non-doctrinal. It avoids or downplays belief requirements in creedal statements and theories developed centuries earlier that are mentally tenuous. Especially to be avoided are the offensive atonement theories that cast God as an angry, vengeful, all-controlling deity, seeking revenge and compensation for human depravity. It is amazing how this message subtly sneaks into Christian liturgy and readings. Its source goes back to the fourth-century doctrine of *original sin*, championed by Augustine. It alone has caused unfathomable harm to individual psyches and harmed the central theme of evolving an ever more perfect humanity.

Anthropomorphism

It is difficult to express the idea of God without reference to anthropomorphism, i.e., human physicality. But efforts should be extended to do so. This also applies to addressing God in gender terms, including father or other terms that have anthropomorphic underpinnings. Consideration should also be given to refashioned modern versions of the Lord's Prayer[4] and other renditions of liturgy and creedal statements.

4. See, for example, *New Zealand Prayer Book*, 181.

Communion

Communion, also known as the Lord's Supper and Eucharist, is a sacrament in the Christian church commemorating Jesus's last meal with his disciples. It is sometimes celebrated weekly, and other times, monthly or less frequently. It is a meaningful expression of the ultimate sacrifice made by Jesus when his life is about to end, his blood spilt, and his body tortured for the sake of humanity's future. The sharing of this sacrament is deeply meaningful for all Christians. For that reason, an open Christian expression avoids lengthy readings and liturgies in the lead up to distributing the bread and wine. Instead, it favors the leader's personal expression of the meaning and context of the original event. The distribution may be by intinction (i.e., dipping the bread in the wine or juice) or other common methods. Substitutes for the words "blood" and "body" may be used if it seems appropriate and in theme but must not diminish the seriousness of the sacrament. The open Christian communion table is open to all.

The Only Way

"I am the way and the truth and the life. No one comes to the Father except through me"[5] has been the justification for Christian exclusivism, pain, and suffering over centuries. Many believe Jesus may have said the first part of this quote, but the second part seems questionable. If we think about the superordinate Christian objective encompassing love of God and neighbor, it is evident that other world religions share it. Open Christianity welcomes insights from other Christian expressions as well as other world and indigenous religions that can provide insight into how best achieve this outcome. Jesus is reported to have said that "whoever is not against us is for us."[6] Hence, contributions furthering Christianity's superordinate objective should not be discounted. The focus should be on the essence, the intent, and action, not on who takes

5. John 14:6.
6. Mark 9:40.

credit for the outcome. In short, the open Christian experience stresses creative expression of the faith and strives for relevance in outcomes, no matter where the help comes from.

Education and Service

An open Christian church values continuing appropriate-level education at all stages of life, from cradle to grave. It inspires and empowers its followers to contribute to the overall good. While it avoids political alliances, it is not hesitant to comment on social immoral stances taken by political factions or to appropriately critique initiatives that strengthen or weaken society's social fabric.

A FINAL WORD

The future of Christianity is uncertain, especially if it continues along the path that it has been on. A case has been made for reform and an open Christianity with a simplistic belief structure for faith has been put forward. Some Christians will embrace this approach, and others may run from it in horror. For the former, open Christianity can be a life-changing faith venture. For the latter, it will likely mean clinging to old Christian practices and belief structures that are unlikely to prevail in the coming decades. It is my hope that a reform like an open Christianity can reinvigorate the Christian church, stir the mystery of faith in the human breast, and in concert with other world religions, lead the human venture into a new age of love, mutual understanding, and human flourishing where being fully human becomes a reality, not just a potential.

THOUGHT EXERCISES

1. Is it possible to pour the new wine into old wineskins? Explain.
2. Have you experienced dissension in church from an attempted reform or other changes? If so, please describe.

3. What parts of the theological perspectives did you find particularly interesting? If so, why?
4. Are there parts of the practical matters you found disturbing? If so, why?
5. How would open Christianity go over in your congregation? What would be the most troublesome parts?

Epilogue

My yoke is easy, and my burden is light.

Matthew 11:30

Christianity has received a wake-up call. It has hemorrhaged followers for over two decades. While the defection has slowed, a substantial remnant remains with tepid enthusiasm. The greatest defection is among younger cohorts, which does not bode well for Christianity in future years. Perhaps, there will be a third *great awakening*. Like the first two, it will need to address the spiritual needs of the populace and, by doing so, usher in a new and powerful ethical revision and challenge to many accepted moral codes. But can that happen without Christianity itself evolving from a tenuous belief-dominated religion into a transcendent faith-based adventure? An open Christianity is a pathway with promise for such an evolution.

The Gospel of Matthew ends with the great commission to make disciples of all nations (i.e., all peoples). Christianity has tried many tactics for achieving this, many of them clearly self-serving and abusive. Through the centuries, Christianity has been reinvigorated by selfless action by those we have designated as saints of the faith. Their approach has not been to *make* disciples but to *inspire* discipleship. That, I believe, is the true interpretation of Matthew's concluding paragraph. By "teaching them to obey everything I have commanded you,"[1] Jesus means following the commandment to love God and neighbor. How to do that is

1. Matt 28:20.

further outlined in his parabolic teachings and his lived example. His yoke is indeed easy and his burdens light, unbridled by creeds, doctrines, ritual, and *correct* yet missing-the-point teaching that is so prevalent in today's Christianity.

Our Christian faith can be a rich map for the maturing of our species and its relationship with the cosmos. Unfortunately, it has too often been hijacked by powerful institutions, charismatic proponents often out for themselves, and a modern mindset that is uncomfortable with mystery. A faith based on the simple concept of love that challenges power and self-aggrandizement has been convoluted into today's complex Christianity. We have taken ancient expressions describing the nature and acts of Jesus and made him a deity with abilities beyond belief. We have confounded our concept of God and exploited it when we no longer can explain the unexplainable. We have taken metaphorical explanations and treated them as factual. It is time to stop all this nonsense and go back to the basics.

The broad message of loving God and neighbor as the basis for a community has been convoluted into a personal message of guilt and personal salvation. Jesus's horizontal concept of the kingdom has been rotated into a vertical religion for appeasing God. A religion of faith has been convoluted into a religion of belief. *An Open Christianity* was written to provide a new start for people who have rejected this, either by leaving Christianity or becoming lukewarm adherents. It is also for those whose faith has plateaued and are seeking more depth in their Christian identity. It has sought to separate the chaff from the grain, the baby from the bath water. It has moved away from treating God and the fully human prototype of Jesus from the bonds of supernaturalism and brought them to us as an ever-present, loving consciousness that is within us, among us, and beyond us. It has sought to again make the Christian journey an adventure.

An open Christianity seeks unity. It espouses not a *here and now* vs. a *hereafter* mindset but one seamless consciousness. It espouses no *sacred* vs. *secular* and no *heaven* vs. *earth* mindset, rather it espouses one holistic cosmos. It espouses no God *out there* but rather a God within us, among us, and, while also present, beyond all. It espouses no supernaturalism, just naturalism. Our cosmos as it exists is beyond all we can understand; it is a miracle unto itself. It is my hope that these writings have opened new vistas for each of your lives and that it may undergird within you a faith that is beyond common reason, born of self-satisfaction, but nevertheless opens a transcendent new world of wonder, life commitment, and excitement.

About the Author

Sam Gould's career spans forty years in corporate management, military service, and academia. In his academic years, he served as a professor of management, director of business research, and dean of business administration. Sam's research has been widely published, and he has consulted with business, government, and nonprofit organizations throughout his career. In his early thirties, Sam began a personal program of in-depth theological study. Since then, he has filled key lay administrative positions and led adult classes across several denominations in the churches he attended. In his job as dean of the school of business administration at a major Catholic university, Sam worked tirelessly to integrate communal Christian themes and ethics into the business school curriculum in new and innovative ways. In retirement, Sam published two previous books, *Faith Beyond Mere Belief* and *Being Christian in the Twenty-First Century*, served on community boards, worked as executive director of a local nonprofit family services organization, and for the past twelve years as chairman of the board of a local community bank. Dr. Gould's formal education includes an undergraduate liberal arts degree from Ohio University, an MBA from the University of Colorado, and PhD in business administration from Michigan State University. He and his wife, Elaine, have been married for sixty-two years and have three married sons and eight grandchildren. Sam and Elaine have resided in Divide, Colorado, for the past twenty years and spend springtime in Santa Fe.

Bibliography

Arnold, Talitha. "Go!" United Church of Christ, Jan. 2, 2024. https://www.ucc.org/daily-devotional/go/.

Astrophotography Lens. "How Far Away Is Alpha Centauri Stars: Distance From Earth in Light Years/Miles/Km." Feb. 23, 2024. https://astrophotographylens.com/blogs/astro/how-far-away-is-alpha-centauri.

Augustine. *St. Augustine of Hippo: The City of God*. Edited by Paul A. Böer. N.p.: Veritatis Splendor, 2012. Kindle ed.

Bader, Christopher, et al. "American Piety in the 21st Century: New Insights to the Depth and Complexity of Religion in the US." Baylor Institute for Studies in Religion, Sept. 2006. https://www.baylor.edu/content/services/document.php/33304.pdf.

Barth, Karl. *The Humanity of God*. Translated by John Newton Thomas and Thomas Wieser. Louisville: Westminster John Knox, 1960.

Bass, Diane Butler. *Christianity After Religion: The End of Church and the Birth of a New Spiritual Awakening*. New York: HarperOne, 2012.

———. *Grounded: Finding God in the World—A Spiritual Revolution*. San Francisco: HarperOne, 2015.

Bethge, Eberhard, ed. *Letters and Papers from Prison*. New York: Touchstone, 1997.

Brenen, Megan. "Belief in Five Spiritual Entities Edges Down to New Lows." Gallup, July 20, 2023. https://news.gallup.com/poll/508886/belief-five-spiritual-entities-edges-down-new-lows.aspx.

Brown, Delwin. *What Does a Progressive Christian Believe? A Guide for the Searching, the Open, and the Curious*. New York: Seabury, 2008.

Bolz-Weber, Nadia. *Shameless: A Sexual Reformation*. New York: Convergent, 2019.

Bonhoeffer, Dietrich. *The Cost of Discipleship*. New York: Macmillan, 1963.

Borg, Marcus. *Speaking Christian: Why Christian Words Have Lost Their Meaning and Power—And How They Can Be Restored*. San Francisco: HarperOne, 2011.

Borg, Marcus J., and John Dominic Crossan. *The First Paul: Reclaiming the Radical Visionary Behind the Church's Conservative Icon*. New York: HarperOne, 2009.

Brueggemann, Walter. *Chosen? Reading the Bible Amid the Israeli-Palestinian Conflict*. Louisville: Westminster John Knox, 2015.

Buber, Martin. *I and Thou*. 2nd ed. Translated by Ronald Gregor Smith. New York: Charles Scribner's Sons, 1958.

Bullivant, Stephen. *Nonverts: The Making of Ex-Christian America*. New York: Oxford University Press, 2022.

Burklo, Jim. *Open Christianity: Home by Another Road*. Haworth, NJ: St. Johann, 2000.

Carr, David M. *The Formation of the Hebrew Bible: A New Reconstruction*. Oxford: Oxford University Press, 2011.

Cobb, John B. Jr., and Clarke H. Pinnock, eds. *Searching for an Adequate God: A Dialogue Between Process and Free Will Theists*. Grand Rapids: Eerdmans, 2000.

Cobb, John B. Jr., and David Ray Griffin. *Process Theology: An Introductory Exposition*. Louisville: Westminster John Knox, 1976.

Colagrossi, Mike. "7 Common Traits of Self-Transcended People: Maslow's Highest Level on the Hierarchy of Needs." Big Think, Feb. 19, 2019. https://bigthink.com/neuropsych/7-traits-self-transcended-people/.

Cooperman, Alan. "Religious 'Switching' Patterns Will Help Determine Christianity's Course in U.S." Pew Research Center, Sept. 29, 2022. https://www.pewresearch.org/short-reads/2022/09/29/religious-switching-patterns-will-help-determine-christianitys-course-in-u-s/.

Cox, Harvey. *The Future of Faith*. New York: HarperOne, 2009.

Cupitt, Don. *The Sea of Faith*. London: SCM, 1994.

Dalberg, John Emerich Edward. "Acton-Creighton Correspondence: Letter I." Cannes, April 5, 1887. https://oll.libertyfund.org/titles/acton-acton-creighton-correspondence.

Davenport, E. R., et al. "The Human Microbiome in Evolution." *BMC Biology* 15.1 (2017) 127. https://link.springer.com/article/10.1186/s12915-017-0454-7.

Davis, James, et al. *The Great Dechurching: Who's Leaving, Why Are They Going, and What Will It Take to Bring Them Back?* Grand Rapids: Zondervan, 2023. Kindle ed.

DeRose, Jason. "Religious 'Nones" Are Now the Largest Single Group in the US." NPR, Jan. 24, 2024. https://www.npr.org/2024/01/24/1226371734/religious-nones-are-now-the-largest-single-group-in-the-u-s.

Dever, William G. *What Did the Biblical Writers Know and When Did They Know It? What Archaeology Can Tell Us About the Reality of Ancient Israel*. Grand Rapids: Eerdmans, 2001.

Deziel, Chris. "Animals that Share Human DNA Sequences." Sciencing, Aug. 30, 2022. https://www.sciencing.com/animals-share-human-dna-sequences-8628167/.

Eckhart, Meister. *The Complete Mystical Works of Meister Eckhart*. Edited and translated by Maurice O'C. Walshe. New York: Crossword, 2009.

Ehrman, Bart D. *God's Problem: How the Bible Fails to Answer Our Most Important Question—Why We Suffer.* San Francisco: HarperOne, 2008.

———. *Jesus, Interrupted: Revealing the Hidden Contradictions in the Bible (and Why We Don't Know About Them).* San Francisco: HarperOne, 2009.

Etzioni, Amitai. *A Comparative Analysis of Complex Organizations.* Revised ed. New York: Free, 1975.

Falk, Harvey. *Jesus the Pharisee: A New Look at the Jewishness of Jesus.* New York: Paulist, 1985.

Feldmeir, Mark. *Life After God: Finding Faith When You Can't Believe Anymore.* Louisville: Westminster John Knox, 2023.

Fox, Matthew. *Original Blessing: A Primer in Creation Spirituality Presented in Four Parts, Twenty-Six Themes, and Two Questions.* New York: Jeremy P. Tarcher/Putnam, 2000.

Francis. "Encyclical Letter *Fratelli Tutti* of the Holy Father Francis on Fraternity and Social Friendship." The Holy See, Oct. 3, 2020. https://www.vatican.va/content/francesco/en/encyclicals/documents/papa-francesco_20201003_enciclica-fratelli-tutti.pdf.

The Gilder Lehrman Institute of American History. "'America the Beautiful,' 1893: A Spotlight on a Primary Source by Katharine Lee Bates." https://www.gilderlehrman.org/history-resources/spotlight-primary-source/america-beautiful-1893.

Goff, Vernon. *Making God Talk Make Sense: A Common Approach to Religion.* Lincoln, NE: Dageforde, 2001.

Gorski, Philip S., and Samuel L. Perry. *The Flag and the Cross: White Christian Nationalism and the Threat to American Democracy.* Oxford: Oxford University Press, 2022. Kindle ed.

Gould, Sam. *Being Christian in the Twenty-First Century.* Eugene, OR: Wipf & Stock, 2017.

———. "An Equity-Exchange Model of Organizational Involvement." *Academy of Management Review* 4 (1979) 53–62.

Greenwood, Kyle. *Scripture and Cosmology: Reading the Bible Between the Ancient World and Modern Science.* Madison: IVP Academic, 2015.

Griffin, Danél F. "My Deconstruction Heroes: John Shelby Spong." Sept. 17, 2021. https://survivingthespirit.com/2021/09/17/my-deconstruction-heroes-john-shelby-spong/.

Gulley, Philip. *If the Church Were Christian: Rediscovering the Values of Jesus.* San Francisco: HarperOne, 2010.

Gulley, Philip, and James Mulholland. *If Grace Is True: Why God Will Save Every Person.* San Francisco: HarperOne, 2003.

Guthrie, Kenneth Sylvan. *The Gospel of Apollonius of Tyana: His Life and Deeds According to Philostratos.* Dublin: Patavium, 2023. Kindle ed.

Hanh, Thich Nhat. *Creating True Peace: Ending Violence in Yourself, Your Family, Your Community, and the World.* New York: Atria, 2003.

Hartshorne, Charles. *The Divine Reality: A Social Conception of God.* New Haven, CT: Yale University Press, 1964.

Hengel, Martin. *Crucifixion in the Ancient World and the Folly of the Message of the Cross*. Philadelphia: Fortress, 1977. Kindle ed.

Hoehn, Richard. *We Carry the Fire: Family and Citizenship as Spiritual Calling*. New York: Church, 2021.

Hout, Michael, and Tom W. Smith. "Fewer Americans Affiliate with Organized Religions, Belief, and Practice Unchanged: Key Findings from the 2014 General Social Survey." NORC, Mar. 10, 2015. https://norc.org/content/dam/norc-org/pdfs/GSS_Religion_2014.pdf.

Irenaeus. *Against Heresies*. Translated by Alexander Roberts and W. H. Rambaut. In *Ante-Nicene Fathers*, vol. 1, edited by Alexander Roberts et al., IV.20.7. Buffalo, NY: Christian Literature, 1885.

Jacobsen, Rowan. "Brains Are Not Required When It Comes to Thinking and Solving Problems—Simple Cells Can Do It." Scientific American, Feb. 1, 2024. https://www.scientificamerican.com/article/brains-are-not-required-when-it-comes-to-thinking-and-solving-problems-simple-cells-can-do-it/.

John of the Cross. *The Collected Works of St. John of the Cross*. Translated by Kieran Kavanaugh and Otilio Rodriguez. Washington, DC: ICS, 1991.

Jones, Jeffrey M. "LGBTQ+ Identification in U.S. Rises to 9.3 Percent." Gallup, Feb. 20, 2025. https://news.gallup.com/poll/656708/lgbtq-identification-rises.aspx.

Jones, Rufus. *A Call to What Is Vital*. New York: Macmillan, 1948.

———. *A Preface to Christian Faith in a New Age*. New York: Macmillan, 1932.

Justice, Ginny. "The Role of Indulgences in the Building of New Saint Peter's Basilica." MLS thesis, Rollins College, 2011. https://scholarship.rollins.edu/mls/7.

Kaufman, Gordon. *An Essay on Theological Method*. 3rd ed. Atlanta: Scholars, 1995.

———. *God the Problem*. Cambridge, MA: Harvard University Press, 1972.

———. *In Face of Mystery: A Constructive Theology*. Cambridge, MA: Harvard University Press, 1993.

Keating, Thomas. *Open Mind, Open Heart: The Contemplative Dimension of the Gospel*. New York: Continuum, 1999.

Kierkegaard, Soren. *A Kierkegaard Anthology*. Edited by Robert Bretall. Princeton: Princeton University Press, 1946.

King, Martin Luther Jr. "Letter from Birmingham Jail." Apr. 16, 1963. https://www.learningforjustice.org/sites/default/files/general/Letter%20from%20Birmingham%20Jail%20MLK.pdf.

King, Robert H. *The Meaning of God*. Philadelphia: Fortress, 1973.

Kennedy, John F. "Inaugural Address, January 20, 1961." JFK Library. https://www.jfklibrary.org/archives/other-resources/john-f-kennedy-speeches/inaugural-address-19610120.

Knitter, Paul F. *Without Buddha, I Could Not Be a Christian*. Oxford: Oneworld, 2009.

Kohanski, Daniel. *A God of Our Invention: How Religion Shaped the Western World*. Hannacroix, NY: Apocryphile, 2023.

Koltko-Rivera, Mark E. "Rediscovering the Later Version of Maslow's Hierarchy of Needs: Self-Transcendence and Opportunities for Theory, Research, and Unification." *Review of General Psychology* 10.4 (2006) 302–17.

Kung, Hans. *On Being Christian*. New York: Image, 1984.

Ladinsky, Daniel. *I Heard God Laughing: Poems of Hope and Joy*. New York: Penguin, 2006.

Lane, Belden C. *Backpacking with the Saints: Wilderness Hiking as Spiritual Practice*. New York: Oxford University Press, 2015.

Lincoln, Abraham. "Gettysburg Address Delivered at Gettysburg Pa. Nov. 19th, 1863." Library of Congress. http://hdl.loc.gov/loc.rbc/rbpe.24404500.

Linn, Jan G. *Unbinding Christianity: Choosing the Values of Jesus over the Beliefs of the Church*. Irvine, CA: Universal, 2020.

Lipka, Michael, and Claire Gecewicz. "More Americans Now Say They're Spiritual but not Religious." Pew Research Center, Sept. 6, 2017. https://www.pewresearch.org/short-reads/2017/09/06/more-americans-now-say-theyre-spiritual-but-not-religious/.

Luther, Martin. "Ninety-Five Theses." Library of Congress. https://www.loc.gov/item/2021667736/.

Marney, Carlyle. *Priests to Each Other*. Valley Forge, PA: Judson, 1974.

Maslow, Abraham H. "A Theory of Human Motivation." *Psychological Review* 50.4 (1943) 370–96.

McEvedy, Colin, and Richard Jones. *Atlas of World Population History*. New York: Puffin, 1978.

McFadden, Robert D. "Amitai Etzioni, 94, Dies; Envisioned a Society Built on the Common Good." *New York Times*, June 17, 2023. https://www.nytimes.com/2023/06/01/us/amitai-etzioni-dead.html.

McLaren, Brian. *Do I Stay Christian? A Guide for the Doubters, the Disappointed, and the Disillusioned*. New York: St. Martin's, 2022.

———. *The Great Spiritual Migration: How the World's Largest Religion Is Seeking a Better Way to Be Christian*. New York: Convergent, 2016.

Mesle, C. Robert. *Process Theology: A Basic Introduction*. St. Louis: Chalice, 1993.

Moody, Edmund R. R., et al. "The Nature of the Last Universal Common Ancestor and Its Impact on the Early Earth System." *Nature Ecology & Evolution* 8 (2024) 1654–66. https://doi.org/10.1038/s41559-024-02461-1.

Mowery, Jeff. "Whiter Than Snow." Hymn of The Week, Aug. 18, 2024. https://hymnoftheweek.net/whiter-than-snow/.

Myers, Robin. *Spiritual Defiance: Building a Beloved Community of Resistance*. New Haven, CT: Yale University Press, 2015.

Nerburn, Kent. *Voices in the Stones: Life Lessons from the Native Way*. Novato, CA: New World Library, 2016.

A New Zealand Prayer Book. Aotearoa, New Zealand: Anglican Church, 1989. https://anglicanprayerbook.nz/.

Newell, John Philip. *The Rebirthing of God: Christianity's Struggle for New Beginnings.* Woodstock, VT: Skylight Paths, 2016.

Niebuhr, Reinhold. *An Interpretation of Christian Ethics.* New York: Harper & Brothers, 1935.

Oord, Thomas Jay, and Tripp Fuller. *God After Deconstruction.* Grasmere, ID: SacraSage, 2024.

Pew Research Center. "About Three-in-Ten U.S. Adults Are Now Religiously Unaffiliated." Dec. 14, 2021. https://www.pewresearch.org/religion/2021/12/14/about-three-in-ten-u-s-adults-are-now-religiously-unaffiliated/.

———. "Decline of Christianity in the U.S. Has Slowed, May Have Leveled Off." Feb. 26, 2025. https://www.pewresearch.org/religion/2025/02/26/decline-of-christianity-in-the-us-has-slowed-may-have-leveled-off/.

———. "Few Americans Blame God or Say Faith Has Been Shaken Amid Pandemic, Other Tragedies." Nov. 23, 2021. https://www.pewresearch.org/religion/2021/11/23/few-americans-blame-god-or-say-faith-has-been-shaken-amid-pandemic-other-tragedies/.

———. "Modeling the Future of Religion in America." Sept. 13, 2022. https://www.pewresearch.org/religion/2022/09/13/modeling-the-future-of-religion-in-america/.

———. "Online Religious Services Appeal to Many Americans but Going in Person Remains More Popular." June 2, 2023. https://www.pewresearch.org/religion/2023/06/02/online-religious-services-appeal-to-many-americans-but-going-in-person-remains-more-popular/.

———. "Religious Landscape Study." https://www.pewresearch.org/religious-landscape-study/.

———. "Religious 'Nones' in America: Who They Are and What They Believe." Jan. 24, 2024. https://www.pewresearch.org/religion/2024/01/24/religious-nones-in-america-who-they-are-and-what-they-believe/.

———. "Why America's 'Nones' Don't Identify with a Religion." Aug. 8, 2018. https://www.pewresearch.org/short-reads/2018/08/08/why-americas-nones-dont-identify-with-a-religion/.

Philostratus. *The Life of Apollonius of Tyana: The Epistles of Apollonius and the Treatise of Eusebius.* Translated by F. C. Conybeare. New York: Macmillan, 1912.

PRRI. "The American Religious Landscape in 2020." Jul. 8, 2021. https://prri.org/research/2020-census-of-american-religion/.

———. "A Christian Nation? Understanding the Threat of Christian Nationalism to American Democracy and Culture." Feb. 8, 2023. https://prri.org/research/a-christian-nation-understanding-the-threat-of-christian-nationalism-to-american-democracy-and-culture/.

———. "PRRI Census of American Religion: County-Level Data on Religious Identity and Diversity." Aug. 29, 2024. https://www.prri.org/research/census-2023-american-religion/.

———. "Religious Change in America." Mar. 27, 2024. https://www.prri.org/research/religious-change-in-america/.

Rasmussen, Larry L. *Earth Honoring Faith: Religious Ethics in a New Key.* New York: Oxford University Press, 2015.

Reber, Arthur S., et al. "The CBC Theory and Its Entailments." *EMBO Reports* 25 (2023) 8–12. https://link.springer.com/article/10.1038/s44319-023-00004-6.

Robert K. Greenleaf Center for Servant Leadership. "What Is Servant Leadership?" https://greenleaf.org/what-is-servant-leadership/.

Robinson, John A. T. *Honest to God.* Philadelphia: Westminster, 1963.

Robinson, John C. *I Am God: Wisdom and Revelation from Mystical Consciousness.* Winchester, UK: John Hunt, 2024.

Roemer, Thomas. *The Invention of God.* Translated by Raymond Guess. Cambridge, MA: Harvard University Press, 2015.

Rohr, Richard. *The Universal Christ: How a Forgotten Reality Can Change Everything We See, Hope for, and Believe.* New York: Convergent, 2021.

Rumi. *The Essential Rumi.* Translated by Coleman Barks. San Francisco: HarperOne, 2004.

Schaff, Phil, ed. *The Complete Works of the Church Fathers.* Delhi: Grapevine, 2016. Kindle ed.

Schillebeeckx, Edward. *Jesus: An Experiment in Christology.* New York: Vintage, 1981.

———. *The Understanding of Faith: Interpretation and Criticism.* New York: Seabury, 1974.

Shea, Mark. "The Dangers of Christian Nationalism." St. Anthony Messenger, Sept. 2024. https://www.franciscanmedia.org/st-anthony-messenger/the-dangers-of-christian-nationalism/.

Sheehan, Thomas. *The First Coming: How the Kingdom of God Became Christianity.* New York: Dorset, 1986.

Shimron, Yonat. "Study: Unaffiliated Americans Are the Only Growing Religious Group." Religion News Service, Mar. 27, 2024. https://religionnews.com/2024/03/27/study-unaffiliated-americans-are-the-only-growing-religious-group/.

Shubin, Neil. *Your Inner Fish: A Journey into the 3.5 Billion Year History of the Human Body.* New York: Vintage, 2009.

Skrbina, David. *Panpsychism in the West.* Cambridge: MIT Press, 2005.

Smith, Huston. *The Illustrated World's Religions: A Guide to Our Wisdom Traditions.* San Francisco: Harper, 1994.

Smith, Mark S. *The Early History of God: Yahweh and the Other Deities in Ancient Israel.* 2nd ed. Grand Rapids: Eerdmans, 2002.

The Socratic Method. "Carol Burnett: 'Giving Birth Is Like Taking Your Lower Lip and Forcing It Over Your Head.'" Sept. 28, 2023. https://www.socratic-method.com/quote-meanings/carol-burnett-giving-birth-is-like-taking-your-lower-lip-and-forcing-it-over-your-head.

Songfacts, "I Write the Songs by Barry Manilow." https://www.songfacts.com/facts/barry-manilow/i-write-the-songs.

Spong, John Shelby. *Biblical Literalism: A Gentile Heresy*. San Francisco: HarperOne, 2016.

———. *Jesus for the Non-Religious*. San Francisco: HarperOne, 2007.

Stark, Rodney. *The Rise of Christianity: How the Obscure, Marginal Jesus Movement Became the Dominant Religious Force in the Western World in a Few Centuries*. San Francisco: HarperOne, 1997.

Stella, Tom. *A Faith Worth Believing: Finding New Life Beyond the Rules of Religion*. San Francisco: HarperOne, 2004.

Taylor, Matthew D. *The Violent Take It by Force: The Christian Movement That Is Threatening Our Democracy*. Minneapolis: Broadleaf, 2024.

Teilhard de Chardin, Pierre. *Christianity and Evolution*. London: Harcourt, Brace, Jovanovich, 1971.

———. *Hymn of the Universe*. New York: Harper & Row, 1965.

Thielen, Martin. "Do You Think I Am Still a Christian?" Doubters Parish, Nov. 1, 2023. https://doubtersparish.com/2023/11/01/do-you-think-i-am-still-a-christian/.

Thurman, Howard. *Jesus and the Disinherited*. Boston: Beacon, 1976.

Tickle, Phyllis. *The Great Emergence: How Christianity Is Changing and Why*. Ada, MI: Baker, 2008.

Tillich, Paul. *The Courage to Be*. New Haven, CT: Yale University Press, 1952.

———. *Dynamics of Faith*. New York: HarperCollins, 1957.

———. *The Shaking of the Foundations*. New York: Charles Scribner's Sons, 1948.

Walters, Kerry, ed. *Rufus Jones Essential Writings*. Maryknoll, NY: Orbis, 2001.

Watts, Alan. *The Wisdom of Insecurity*. New York: Vantage, 1951.

Wilkerson, Isabel. *Caste: The Origins of Our Discontent*. New York: Random House, 2020.

Wink, Walter. *The Human Being: Jesus and the Enigma of the Son of the Man*. Minneapolis: Fortress, 2002.

Yoder, John Howard. *The Politics of Jesus*. Grand Rapids: Eerdmans, 1972.

www.ingramcontent.com/pod-product-compliance
Lightning Source LLC
LaVergne TN
LVHW012333100826
845148LV00017B/2130

* 9 7 9 8 3 8 5 2 7 2 1 6 7 *